Happy Indian Cooking

best

Torie Two

CHILLI & MINT

INDIAN HOME COOKING FROM A BRITISH KITCHEN

TORIE TRUE

Contents

Breakfasts

Snacks and Salads

Dals and Soups

Vegetables

Introduction

I am a bit of an anomaly. I am entirely British, a native of these isles, and have for some time run successful courses teaching people how to cook home-style Indian food. Sure, we are all global citizens now, but in my case, I guess it was triggered by meeting and then marrying my husband. He was born in Kolkata and came to the UK as a young boy. His family, like all Indian families I know, have a strong culinary tradition, appreciate good food and are all adept in the kitchen. I watched, I noted, I tried, I failed, I tried again and got the hang of it and then the addiction. Combine that with visits to India over the decades plus a healthy dose of curiosity and soon enough my friends were all hankering for invitations to dinner. Then came the inevitable interrogations as to how all these ubiquitous British ingredients tasted so good, followed by my blog, Chilli and Mint, and the cooking classes. I was a working mother, I juggled it all and this was a great way of creating something wonderful, with surprisingly good results once the basics were orientated.

I love the fact that Indian food, much like Indian life, is so filled with colour. We eat with our eyes before any food even goes near our mouths and eating a plate of Indian food really is like eating the rainbow. It releases happy endorphins, which only heighten when you taste the glorious flavours. Travels to India further fuelled my enthusiasm for the cuisine, the culture, and the people. I urge everyone to visit once in their lifetime if they can. Stepping off a plane and landing on Indian soil, I always feel as if I have entered a world where the lights have been turned on as everything is so vivid and one's senses are heightened to the extreme. It's intoxicating despite the heat and non-stop frenzy of activity, and I always feel my most alive when I am there. Everyday life is played out before you like a living theatre that you can't help but be entranced by.

Growing up in rural Sussex couldn't have been further removed from life in India. My family had a deep respect for the country though, my parents having travelled there in the early 1970s, and my grandmother worked for the Indian embassy for many years. One similarity when it came to food, however, was that my mother made delicious, homecooked meals every day. Microwave dinners just didn't feature; in fact we didn't even own a microwave. What we were fortunate to have was the most bountiful vegetable garden and fruit orchard, providing my family with runner beans, redcurrants and blackcurrants, potatoes, marrows, courgettes, onions, leeks, strawberries, raspberries, carrots, damsons, golden gages (my favourite), Victoria plums, apples, pears, figs… you name it, it grew with abundance. It was all very bucolic and delicious with no plastic in sight.

Spices in the 1980s were not as commonplace and understood as they are today in modern Britain. I recall my mother having a small collection of spices including the standard curry powder, ground cumin, cinnamon and turmeric, cinnamon quills, cardamom pods, and cumin and coriander seeds, but knowing how to use them was limited to a few books that had been written on the subject. Knowing where to begin for the uninitiated was daunting and only the very enthusiastic would delve into the subject of spice. If you wanted curry, you would head to your local curry house or have take-out, where creamy, rich and spicy curries were made for the British palate.

Most people I meet love Indian food and would like to have more of it in their diet, but just don't know how to go about doing this. For some reason there seems to be a mental block that tells us cooking with spice is difficult, which really does not need to be the case in most instances. By learning a few tips and tricks you can bring Indian cuisine into your weekly meals. If you want more vegetarian or vegan meals, then Indian cuisine is a great way to achieve it; after all, most Indian people in India eat mainly vegetarian food. It's super nutritious and, as we are increasingly learning, has a whole host of health benefits, feeds plenty of people and is cost effective. Meat and fish are reserved for special occasions and not eaten as frequently as they are in the West. So, while my book is not exclusively vegetarian, my largest chapter is on vegetable dishes that will hopefully excite and satisfy in equal measure.

Many of the meat curries in this book can also be made with paneer, tofu, or cauliflower to make them vegetarian or vegan. The recipes are not long-winded and cumbersome. Yes, you need to have a few spices in your store cupboard to get going – like a painter would need paints before painting their canvas – but you don't need too many, and you may well find that you have some already waiting to be used up.

Many of my live cooking classes, pre-covid, included a short tour of a local Asian area near to where I live. I found this really encouraged, inspired and helped my clients to know which spices to buy and where to purchase them. They could see the wide range of produce on offer, as well as shops selling all manner of pots, pans, tiffin boxes and other kitchen gadgets useful for Indian cooking. We would then have a brief stop for some Indian snacks to refuel – with chilli-stuffed pakora appealing to the most adventurous – before returning to my house to start cooking. To help guide you with spices in this book, I have put together a section which tells you about the spices you can begin to build up in your store cupboard (see page 10), as well as a section on suppliers (see page 228), which I hope will help give you an idea on where to purchase them easily.

Many of the recipes within this book are ones that I teach in my classes (both live and, over much of 2020 and 2021, on Zoom) so they have been tried and tested numerous times and ultimately work. You are unlikely to find any standard curry house favourites in this book. Chicken tikka masala, butter chicken and dal makhana do not feature. Instead, these are the recipes that people cook regularly in the home to feed and nourish their loved ones. They are accessible and most are not tricky, so hopefully they will encourage you to bring a little more spice into your culinary repertoire. Be brave, be bold and give it a go. A whole new world awaits your tastebuds.

Store Cupboard Spices

There are so many wonderful spices out there that it can seem a bit overwhelming to someone who hasn't grown up around spices or isn't used to cooking with them on a regular basis. I felt it would be helpful to list the ones that I use most often, along with some information about the spice itself. As far as storage is concerned, I would suggest buying smaller packets and then transferring the contents into airtight glass containers; old jam jars work perfectly well. Place them somewhere cool, out of direct sunlight and where no moisture can get to them. They are best used within 6 months.

Ajwain Seeds (Carom Seeds)

These have a very similar oval shape to fennel and cumin seeds, but with a slightly more ridged texture. They contain a compound called thymol, which can also be found in thyme, hence they can offer a similar taste. Ajwain can make a powerful statement though, so you only need a small amount to bring out the taste. They are great in fried snacks, such as pakora, and Indian breads.

Asafoetida (Hing)

Also referred to as 'devils' dung stinking gum', this sunshine-yellow spice is the dried gum or resin from the sap of the roots of a plant in the fennel family. The 'stinking gum' name refers to its pungent smell, which dissipates completely when it is cooked in a little oil. It then takes on an onion-garlic aroma and is often used as a substitute for onions and garlic by Jains and some Brahmins who generally avoid eating these ingredients. For the former, this is because they come from the soil and the whole plant is killed in order to consume them, and the latter believe that onion and garlic release our inner passions. Asafoetida is sold in powdered or granular form; I always opt for the powdered variety. You only ever need to add a pinch to a dish, never more than quarter of a teaspoon. Less is more with this spice.

Bengali Five Spice (Panch Phoron)

Not to be confused with Chinese five spice, this Bengali blend is made up of almost equal parts nigella, cumin, fennel, black mustard and fenugreek seeds. It is only really found in dishes from East India. In Kolkata, where my husband was born, and where we have a lot of family members, it is used a lot. Panch phoron is the spice mix that I use in my cherry tomato masoor dal on page 70 and my Bengali lamb chop curry on page 148.

Black Peppercorns

Known as black gold, pepper ruled long before chilli had been introduced to India. The Portuguese brought this powerful spice in the 15th century, and it has continued to thrive in South India's Malabar coast ever since. One of my favourite curries gives black pepper a shining role: the South Indian chettinad pepper chicken (see page 150). Pepper has a very different heat to chilli, is similarly robust and dances around the tongue with great gusto. White, green and black peppercorns all come from same plant, Piper Nigrum, but pink peppercorns are from a different plant entirely. As black pepper dries out it ignites a reaction that creates piperine, the active ingredient in pepper. It's always best to freshly grind any peppercorns as and when you require them for your curries.

Black Salt (Kala Namak)

One of the more obscure ingredients in the spice cupboard, black salt has a very distinct umami taste and a sulphurous aroma, like hard-boiled eggs. A little completely transforms my tamarind sharbat recipe (see page 200) and works so well with the sour notes from the tamarind. In Ayurveda – the ancient Indian medical system – black salt is considered a cooling spice.

Cardamom, Green and Black

My favourite aromatic spice, which has two varieties that are very different in appearance and taste. The more ubiquitous is the green cardamom pods, which are used in both sweet and savoury dishes. You can open the pod to release the seeds, or you can add the whole pod to a curry. Less well known are the black cardamom pods, which are a lot bigger than the green and only used in savoury dishes. They look more like a dark brown nut, similar to a nutmeg. You would tend to use only a couple, at most, in a curry, whereas you may use three times that amount for the green cardamom. Black cardamom is smoky and reminds me of lapsang souchong tea. They work really well with meat curries, giving the whole dish a smoky edge.

Chaat Masala

Chaat (or chat) is the term given to Indian snacks and appetisers. Chaat masala is my absolute favourite masala; it is so versatile and a taste sensation overloaded with sweet, sour and salty notes. It includes a whole medley of spices and seasonings including mango powder, black salt, cumin, black pepper, dried mint, asafoetida, cloves, coriander, dried ginger, chilli powder, sugar and salt. The masala works equally well with fruit and vegetables, so you'll find it makes many appearances in this book, from the chaat salad (see page 56) to daler bora (see page 46) and sweet potato tikki (see page 50) as well as in my green mung, garlic and tomato dal on page 72 which is not a traditional addition, but one that I have adapted as I think it works so well.

Chilli Powder

I mostly use Kashmiri chilli powder, which has a vibrant red colour and a mild heat, so is the perfect addition to some curries. It is made from ground dried Kashmiri chillies and is not the same as paprika or cayenne pepper. When I want a hotter chilli powder, I opt for the one simply called 'chilli powder' which you can find in all Asian grocery stores and some of the larger supermarkets. It is often a more muted red colour but is a lot hotter so use with caution. I would suggest halving the amount you add to a recipe if you do not have Kashmiri chilli powder and are using an alternative.

Cinnamon (Dalchini)

Cinnamon is a deliciously sweet spice that comes from the inner bark of the Cinnamomum tree. There are in fact two types of cinnamon; 'true cinnamon' is grown in Sri Lanka and less well known in the UK. The other type is 'cassia cinnamon' which comes from the Cinnamomum cassis tree, originating from southern China and hence also referred to as Chinese cinnamon. On close inspection they look slightly different, and their essential oil makeup varies hugely. True cinnamon is lighter in colour and the inner bark is stripped and dried to form thin paper layers coiled around each other. These are called cinnamon sticks or quills. Cassia cinnamon is a darker brown colour and is thicker with a rougher, woodier texture than the Sri Lankan variety. The cassia variety has the stronger flavour and is most commonly consumed around the world. For most of my dishes, I cook with the whole spice instead of its powdered form. You can use either cinnamon sticks or cassia bark in my recipes, whichever you find easiest to source.

Cloves

Cloves remind me of winter baking and mulled wine, but they are also commonly used in Indian cuisine, both savoury and sweet. You only need a few, so as to not overpower the whole dish. They look like little brown nails, which is where their name derives from: the word clou in French means nail. The clove is a deep pink flower, which is picked just before it opens and then dried, darkening its appearance. Medicinally, they are said to be good for toothache.

Coriander (Dhaniya)

Coriander also comes in seed and powdered form. It tastes very different to fresh coriander, which I discuss in the fresh ingredients section on page 20. The dried spice has mellow floral and citrus notes and is often found in dishes across Asia and the Middle East. When whole, it is a light brownish yellow round seed and is great for pickling. Like all spices, you need to toast them over a medium heat to release all their wonderful aromas. Do this before grinding them into a fine powder if you are making your own ground coriander. Coriander is said to be very good for treating digestive issues.

Cumin (Jeera)

Cumin comes in seed and powdered form and the seeds themselves range in colour from a light green through to brown and black. Cumin has a very distinctive flavour that could be described as smoky, nutty and warming. The aroma strengthens further when it is roasted or heated in hot oil; black cumin has the most intense smoky aroma. You can make the powdered form yourself or buy it ready-made. The powdered form is always a darker brown in colour than coriander powder but not as dark as garam masala powder. You will find it often partnered with ground coriander and ground turmeric; in many respects these are the 'Three Musketeers' of spices.

Dried Fenugreek Leaves (Kasoori Methi)

You can of course buy fresh fenugreek leaves to make a wonderful shaak or sabzi, but they are hard to source unless you live near an Asian grocer, so I have only included one recipe with them in this book (my fenugreek lamb curry on page 156), although you can substitute with dried for that dish. The dried leaves are easy to find online and in large supermarkets. They have a very distinct aroma, which works particularly well in my cauliflower and potato curry (see page 108), chicken methi malai (see page 154) and Punjabi chole (see page 82). It is always best to crumble them as you sprinkle them over your meat and vegetables to release their wonderful aroma.

Dried Mango Powder (Amchoor)

This powder is made of unripe green mangoes, giving it a sour and tart zing. Perfect for sprinkling over Indian snacks.

Fennel Seeds

Similar looking to cumin seeds but slightly larger, with a light green hue and a delicate aniseed flavour. They work equally well with sweet and savoury dishes. They are also one of the five ingredients in the Bengali five spice known as panch phoron.

Fenugreek Seeds (Methi)

Small, golden brown, angular seeds that have a bitter taste, so they need to be used sparingly. They are only used in savoury dishes and again are part of the Bengali panch phoron spice blend. They are often used in pickling, as well as for enhancing meat and vegetable dishes.

Garam Masala

Wonderfully warming spices that you can use whole or more commonly ground. I only use the ground version at the end of a dish, giving added complexity and warmth. Typically, black pepper, cumin seeds, coriander seeds, cinnamon bark, cloves, mace, fennel seeds, green cardamom and bay leaves are used, although in Bengal the standard garam masala uses only three spices: green cardamom, cinnamon bark and cloves. Each Indian household has their own version so play around with these spices and create your own. Store-bought garam masala powder is good too and I tend to opt for this on most occasions.

Mustard Seeds (Rai)

Mustard seeds come in shades of black, brown and yellow and it's black and brown that are most commonly used in Indian cuisine. They share the same characteristics, although the black seeds are slightly larger. Be careful when cooking with them as they do tend to pop when tempered in oil. In Bengal, the mustard seed is king and is used in a wide variety of dishes with fish and vegetables, and also made into a paste. The oil is also commonly used in Bengali cooking, which has a pungent smell, so make sure you have an extractor fan on if using.

Nigella Seeds (Kalonji/Black Onion Seeds)

The nigella seed comes from a flowering plant – Nigella Sativa – that belongs to the onion family. In each petal of the flower a few seeds are found. While the black seeds are tiny, they are big on flavour with a strong smoky aroma and nutty flavour. They are always kept whole and are used in a myriad of curries, dals and salads. I also love to scatter them on top of homemade naan bread.

Poppy Seeds (Posto)

These come from the opium poppy in shades of white, black or blue. Please note that those used for culinary purposes have none of the alkaloids associated with the narcotic. I mainly use white poppy seeds in my cooking for a nutty flavour and texture. In Bengali cuisine these are called posto and get star treatment in many dishes. You'll find them in my appropriately named opium chicken on page 170 and also on my fried white poppy seed aubergine on page 44.

Star Anise

Shaped like a star as the name suggests, this spice is not only used in Chinese cuisine but also Indian. It is dark brown in appearance and often has eight points. It is used in both sweet and savoury dishes, giving them a powerful aniseed aroma.

Turmeric (Haldi)

The most ubiquitous of Indian spices and one that I use in pretty much all my curries. It is easily identifiable by its vibrant yellow colour, owing to a pigment known as curcumin. I mainly use it in powdered form for ease, instead of the fresh turmeric root which looks like gnarly ginger. That said, fresh turmeric is great thinly sliced and added to boiling water with some lemon juice and black pepper to help with its absorption, as a drink to be gently sipped. Turmeric has an earthy aroma and should be used sparingly or else you will end up with a bitter tasting dish. Most of my recipes require no more than a teaspoon of ground turmeric. It has a plethora of health benefits, including being anti-carcinogenic, antiseptic, anti-inflammatory, good for digestion and immune boosting.

Lentils/Dal/Legume

Lentils – also referred to as dal or legume – are a mainstay in the Indian diet. When I am in India, I eat them every day in some form. Back in the UK I eat them on average three times a week. High in protein and fibre, they are low in fat and are essentially a superfood. There are so many ways to eat them, as you will see in my chapter dedicated to Dals and Soups from page 60.

How watery or not you like your dal is completely up to you. I never measure out the water, instead relying on the Indian art of approximation, known as andaaz. However, in these recipes I do give you guidance on how much water to add. As you become conversant with dals, feel free to alter the amount of water you add to suit your preferences.

Please note that this list only includes lentils used within this book.

Black-Eyed Beans/Peas (Lobia or Rongi or Chawli)

I use the jarred or tinned variety of these to save a lot of time for the same reasons as red kidney beans. They are delicious in my tamarind and coconut curry on page 64.

Chana Dal (Bengal Gram or Split Chickpeas)

Chana dal is yellow in colour and slightly larger than toor dal. Chana dal comes from black chickpeas that are split and the outer husk is removed to reveal the yellow chana. You can soak or cook without soaking, though I tend to opt for the former to reduce the cooking time and aid digestion. They take around the same time to cook as toor, so 40-50 minutes. See my coconut and sultana chana dal on page 66.

Chickpeas (Chana)

Chickpeas should not be confused with chana dal, which are split chickpeas. Chickpeas are kept whole to make a much-loved dal known as chole and chana masala. It can be confusing but the only recipes in this book that I use whole chickpeas for are the Punjabi chole on page 82 and chaat salad on page 56. I also buy jarred or tinned chickpeas for speed and convenience. If you are using the dried variety, you must soak them overnight and then boil them for over an hour until soft.

Green Mung/Moong Beans (Green Gram)

I would recommend soaking these for a minimum of 5 hours or overnight. If you soak them overnight you can begin to make mung bean sprouts which require draining to get rid of any excess water, then placing in a partially covered bowl in a dark, warm place. After a further 12 hours, sprouts will begin to push through. You can then make them into a delicious salad. To make regular dal you need to boil the green mung for around 30 minutes on a medium to high heat. Again, it depends on the brand you buy so it may take a little longer. See my green mung, garlic and tomato dal on page 72.

Red Kidney Beans (Rajma)

When dry, these beans need to be soaked overnight and then boiled for over an hour. I don't use the dried version, instead opting for the ones in jars or tins, found in Asian grocers or large supermarkets, which taste good and save a lot of time and soaking. They are delicious in my rajma recipe on page 74.

Red Split Lentils (Masoor Dal)

This is the most ubiquitous of lentils and easy to source in most grocers, stores and supermarkets. They do not require soaking and are the quickest to cook, ready within 15 minutes. Orange in colour, they become yellow and soften during cooking. Any of my recipes that require yellow moong/mung dal can be substituted with red split lentils. See my cherry tomato masoor dal on page 70, Sri Lankan coconut dal on page 85 and daler bora (red split lentil fritters) on page 46.

Toor Dal (Split Pigeon Peas)

Toor looks very similar to chana dal but is slightly smaller and more regular in shape. You can soak it to speed up the cooking time, but this is not essential. Toor is larger in size than both red split and yellow mung dal, so takes around 40-50 minutes to soften. It's used to make the sambar on page 86 as well as my dhaba style dal fry on page 62.

White Urid Dal (Split Black Gram)

Be mindful that there is also black urid dal, known as black gram. In this book, I use white urid dal which are also referred to as split black gram. I use them to make one of my favourite Indian snacks, known as savoury doughnuts or medu vada, on page 52. They do require soaking for a minimum of 4 hours.

Yellow Moong/Mung (Yellow Split Peas)

These small yellow lentils are the second quickest to cook. They are easy to source in most grocers and supermarkets. Typically, they are cooked within 25 minutes, but sometimes, depending on the brand, they may take a little longer. You can cook without soaking but soaking even for a short while will speed up the cooking time. These can easily be substituted with red split lentils. See my recipes for butternut yellow mung dal on page 84, dhaba style dal fry on page 62 and palak dal on page 78.

Fresh Ingredients

It is becoming easier than ever to source fresh ingredients that are used in Indian cuisine. I have steered you towards recipes that incorporate vegetables which are broadly available, so if you do live near an Asian grocer, you may note the absence of such vegetables as karela (bitter melon), tindora (gentleman's toes) and ribbed gourd (turia) in this book. These are less widely available outside specialist suppliers, so I have avoided using them in my recipes.

Coriander Leaves

Coriander is without doubt a core herb for me. Use the leaves and stalks; the latter add a huge amount of flavour when finely chopped and added to curries and dals. If a bunch of coriander is looking tired, make up some of my coriander, mint and lime chutney on page 192 which works well with most things, even if you are going to simply grill some fish or chicken.

Curry Leaves

I highly recommend sourcing fresh curry leaves if you can. They can be found in some of the large supermarkets, as well as a host of Asian grocers. I store mine by freezing them and then cooking with them from frozen as and when I require them. They will last many months this way and still taste great. Dried curry leaves can be used but lack the flavour of fresh or frozen.

Dill Leaves

Dill is not identified as a herb used in Indian food but dill leaves are used in some dals (see my dill dal on page 80). Dill is readily available at all large supermarkets as well as local Asian grocers.

Fresh Chillies

There are numerous chillies from around the world with different flavours. I tend to use the long thin green chillies, which in the Asian grocers are simply called green chillies. They are larger than the Thai green chillies, which are super-hot, but a lot thinner and indeed hotter than the more bulbous chillies such as jalapeño. If I buy a lot, I freeze them and then use them from frozen when required. For these recipes, buy whichever chillies you like to use and you are comfortable eating. The trick is to taste all the beautiful flavours of the dishes without overpowering them with chilli. When starting out, err on the side of caution and use perhaps half a chilli with the seeds removed and then next time try leaving the seeds in. Adjust amounts to your own individual requirements.

Jaggery

Strictly speaking, jaggery is not a fresh ingredient. It is a natural alternative to sugar, brown in colour, and is used across the Indian subcontinent, Southeast Asia and Africa. It is made from unrefined sugar cane and is used as a sweetener in Indian desserts and some curries. It is like molasses and can be purchased in block form or cubes that you can then break down. You can use brown sugar as a substitute, so it isn't essential for any of the recipes in this book, but it is a nice addition to some of the dishes if you chance upon it.

Methi/Fenugreek Leaves

I only have one recipe in here that requires fresh fenugreek leaves, so if you come across them on your travels do pick up a bunch and then make my fenugreek lamb curry on page 156. They are super nutritious and a great addition to your diet. They have small, green, teardrop-shaped leaves, which you remove from the stalks and use only the leaves in the curry. I use the dried variety more regularly. When you add these into a curry, you need to break them up in your hand, releasing their fragrance as you do so. You'll find them in my chicken methi malai on page 154 and my cauliflower and potato curry on page 108.

Moringa/Drumstick

I have included the option to incorporate drumstick in two recipes (sambar on page 86 and avial on page 124). You absolutely don't have to include them but if you come across them while shopping then you know what to make! Drumsticks look like their namesake and are as long as the real thing, with grooves along their sides.

Pandan Leaves

These fragrant leaves completely transform South Indian and Sri Lankan dishes. They are also found in many Thai sweet and savoury dishes. Asian grocers (see the suppliers section on page 228) are often a good place to look for them. The leaves are long and slender with a tipped end. Like curry leaves, I freeze mine and then cook them from frozen. I cut them down to 3 inches in length and halve them down the middle. The recipes that include them are the beetroot curry on page 98, Sri Lankan coconut dal on page 85 and spicy caramelised onion sambol on page 191.

Tamarind

The tamarind tree produces brown pod-like fruit whose seeds and pulp are used to make tamarind paste. It's deliciously sour, tangy and sweet and gives a great balance to a few dishes in this book. Typically, I buy it in block form, which is now easily available, then take off a golf ball sized piece (which is around 45-50g) and place it in a small bowl, cover with boiling water and leave it to break down and loosen over 15 minutes. Break it down further with a spoon or, as the water cools, with your hand. Then it is simply a case of straining it, using a spoon to push all the paste through the sieve. You then discard any stones or fibres left in the strainer and use both the tamarind paste and liquid in the recipe. You can use tamarind concentrate paste, but this is a lot stronger and ranges from brand to brand, hence I have said to use between 1 and 2 teaspoons as an equivalent. My advice would be to use a teaspoon, then after a little cooking to taste test and decide whether it requires an extra teaspoon to give more sour notes. Both block form and concentrate paste should be stored in the fridge once opened.

Kitchen Equipment

Some of the best food I have eaten around the world has come from the humblest of kitchens or street stalls, where flavours have been conjured up with relatively few utensils. So, I truly believe that incredible food can come from the most basic set ups. In the West, we tend to fill our kitchens with many gadgets that we seldom use. While pressure cookers are sometimes used in India to make dals and some curries, in the West they are not so commonly used so I have not included them in this section or used them to make any recipes in this book. The list below is what I use to cook all the dishes in this book on a regular basis. I have not included chopping boards and stirring spoons but it goes without saying that you will need these too.

Appam/Hoppers Pan

I have the non-stick versions, which are easier to use than the traditional cast iron ones. I do have a couple so I can make appams/hoppers simultaneously but when starting out, you only need one.

Handheld Grater

I find my large Prestige handheld grater hugely useful for finely grating my ginger and garlic.

Indian Kadai/Karahi

These saucepans are commonly used in India; they are wide, deep and are the Indian version of a wok. I do have a couple of traditional Indian ones, but also have similar non-stick versions which I picked up at a British supermarket that has a kitchen equipment section. Make sure you buy one with a lid. I also find my cast iron casserole pot is brilliant for cooking curries.

Knives

It goes without saying that you need a couple of good sharp knives to prepare your vegetables, dice your meat and cut your fish. Keep them sharp and store them safely. A good value brand which I use is Victorinox.

Pestle and Mortar

I picked up my beautiful marble pestle and mortar from Mr Patel who runs Little India at 191 Upper Tooting Road, London. It's quite large and a statement piece in my kitchen. His shop is a treasure trove of kitchen equipment and incense, well worth a visit if you are in the area. You can buy most of the items listed here from him easily.

Slotted Spoon

Necessary for removing fried snacks from oil. Metal rather than plastic is best for obvious reasons!

Spice Grinder and Chopper

Make sure you buy a spice grinder that is easy to clean. Mine comes with a separate grinder and chopper attachment and is under £30. I find it hugely useful to make speedy spice masalas or to blend individual spices in my grinder and chutneys in my chopper. The contraption is relatively small so is easy to store. Some coffee grinders are good for blending spices, but make sure you can properly clean it, otherwise your coffee may take on interesting new flavours!

Stainless Steel Spice Box

I keep most of my spices in glass jars in a cool, dark room but I do have a couple of spice boxes near my stove which I use daily. These contain my most used spices in smaller proportions which saves me retrieving the larger containers every time I cook. When you start out, I think this particular piece of equipment is unnecessary; you can just use old glass jars with secure lids instead.

Tawa

While I do have a few tawas – a flat frying pan – to cook my chapati, naan and paratha, a regular large non-stick frying pan will do an equally good job.

Wooden Spatula

Very useful for turning over Indian flatbreads. You do not want to use metal instruments on metal pans, especially if they are non-stick.

Author's Notes

An Indian meal: An Indian meal is different from your typical meal in the West, in that dishes are eaten in a particular order. In the West, we might put our protein and vegetables on the same plate. However, when I eat with my Indian family members, we start with a little dal and rice or flatbreads, then we proceed to one or two vegetable curries. Following this there may be a fish dish or a meat curry. We would then finish with a sweet palate cleanser such as fresh mango, when in season. So, we have lots of little portions – like Spanish tapas – over the course of the meal.

Dal: How you like your dal is up to you. You may prefer a soupy or thick consistency, like porridge. I tend to gravitate slightly more towards the former, but it is totally down to personal preference. At the temples in India, thousands are fed vegan food each day if they show up at the right time. The dal is watery but works so well poured over a little rice. The ratio of water to lentils varies between 300-400ml of water to every 100g of lentils, depending on the type of lentils. Play around with these ratios and decide which consistency you prefer. There is no right or wrong answer.

Ginger and garlic: I tend to use fresh garlic and ginger in my recipes, either finely chopping or grating them as required. However, for ease and speed I do use the store-bought pastes occasionally. Personally, I like the Sapna brand, but use whichever you can find. I would avoid the chopped garlic that comes in vinegar though, as that will not work well. I have included a recipe for ginger and garlic paste in this book (see page 220), which is frozen into cubes and used from frozen. Alternatively, finely grating equal amounts of ginger and garlic and then mixing them together will give you the same end result.

Leaving out a spice: If you don't have a particular spice for a dish – asafoetida, for example – simply leave it out. The dish will still taste wonderful. Do check my list of suppliers on page 228 though, which will help you build up your spice store cupboard.

Leftovers: The meat, fish and vegetable curries and dals are all great as leftovers, sometimes tasting even better, and will last in the fridge for a few days. You can also freeze them.

Onions: For all the recipes in this book you can use white or red onions. I have given my preference for some recipes, but if you have only one variety then use that. They are all interchangeable.

Oven temperatures: Please note I use a fan oven so 180°C fan equates to 200°C in a conventional oven or 400°F, and Gas Mark 6. All conversions are given on recipes that use an oven.

Portion size: The recipes in this book are usually for 4 or 4-6 people, unless otherwise specified. When I say 4-6, this means it will feed 4 (with rice or Indian flatbread as an accompaniment) or 6 if the dish is served with a couple of other dishes. I typically always cook a little more than I would need as nearly all the recipes make great leftovers, most freeze well, and you never know when an extra guest may pop by.

Salt: For most of the recipes I have stated 'I tsp, or to taste'. Salt is vital for bringing out the flavours in dals, curries and street snacks, but some salts taste saltier than others. I tend to use table salt for cooking Indian food, as opposed to salt flakes, but adjust accordingly depending on what salt you use and how salty you like your food. It is also best to add a little at first, and then add more if required after you have tasted the dish. If you ever accidentally oversalt, put a whole peeled potato in your pot and leave it in there during the duration of the cooking. Remove at the end and it will have absorbed a lot of the salt. Lemon also helps to balance things out well.

BREAKFASTS

In India, breakfasts are worth getting out of bed for. The options are limitless and what you will be given depends on where you are in the country. In the north, Indian flatbreads such as paratha and chapati are served with light vegetable dishes, or you may get pudla – chickpea pancakes – with some chutney. Batura is another northern classic to be enjoyed with chole. Head further south and the breakfasts are more rice or semolina based. You will come across appam, dosa, pongal, upma and medu vada. Usually these are served with chutney or a small bowl of sambar on the side.

Chickpea Pancakes

Preparation time: 10 minutes
Cooking time: 10-15 minutes
Makes 5 (or more if smaller)

150g gram/chickpea flour

1 tsp salt, or to taste

200ml water

1 tsp ajwain/carom seeds

¼ tsp ground turmeric

20g fresh coriander, finely chopped

1 fresh green chilli, finely chopped (optional)

1 large tomato

½ small red or white onion

1 tbsp vegetable or rapeseed oil

Chickpea pancakes are commonly found in North India and are often referred to as pudla, cheela or chilla. These protein-rich and gluten-free pancakes are made with chickpea flour (also known as gram flour). They are perfect for breakfast as they are speedy to prepare and cook, but are equally appetising for lunch or a light supper too. Getting the texture right is key. You want to aim for a pancake batter consistency: not too thick, not too runny. They are not unlike a dosa though smaller; aim for the size of a side plate.

1. Place the flour and salt into a bowl (no need to sieve them) and gradually add the water while whisking until the mixture is smooth and the consistency of a normal pancake batter. If it becomes too thin, just add a little extra chickpea flour.

2. Add the ajwain, ground turmeric, fresh coriander and green chilli, if using, to the bowl and stir them into the batter.

3. Roughly chop the tomato and onion, place them into a blender and blitz until smooth, then add this paste to the batter.

4. Heat a non-stick frying pan or tawa and grease with some of the oil, making sure the whole surface is covered. Add one ladleful of batter and gently smooth it out into a circle using the back of the ladle. Aim to make the pancakes around 15cm (6 inches) in diameter.

5. Keep the heat low and gently cook the pancake until small bubbles appear on the surface. Use a spatula to make sure the pancake does not stick and to check it is nicely bronzing.

6. When the underside is lightly bronzed, use a spatula to turn over the pancake. Cook for a further minute while checking that side is also bronzing.

7. Once both sides are nicely bronzed, remove the pancake from the pan and serve up. Repeat the cooking process with the rest of the batter.

Notes: These go really well with my Bengali tomato chutney (see page 191). If you eat them for lunch or supper, a simple rocket or watercress salad makes a lovely side.

Aloo Bhaji – Spiced Potato

Preparation time: 15 minutes
Cooking time: 20 minutes
Serves 6

800g potatoes, peeled

2 tbsp vegetable or rapeseed oil

1 tsp ghee (optional)

1 tsp black or brown mustard seeds

1 tbsp white urid lentils/dal

1 tbsp chana lentils/dal

2 tbsp cashews or peanuts, roughly chopped

¼ tsp asafoetida powder

10-15 curry leaves

2 fresh green chillies, finely sliced

1 white or red onion, finely chopped

1 heaped tsp finely grated fresh ginger or ginger paste

1 heaped tsp finely grated garlic or garlic paste

½ tsp ground turmeric

1 tsp salt, or to taste

1 tsp caster sugar

200ml water

Fresh coriander leaves, to garnish (optional)

This spiced potato, or aloo bhaji as it is commonly known in India, is the perfect filling for masala dosas, samosas, potato bonda and stuffed paratha. It's so tasty you can even eat it as a dish on its own. As it is so versatile, it is a great one to have in your Indian culinary arsenal.

1. Begin by boiling the potatoes in a pan of water until soft. Drain and mash them, then set aside to cool.

2. Heat the oil and ghee, if using, in a pan and then add the mustard seeds, white urid and chana lentils. They will add texture and a little bite to the dish, which works well. You cannot eat them raw but cooking them in hot oil makes them edible. Gently move the lentils and mustard seeds around in the oil for 30 seconds and then add the nuts, asafoetida, curry leaves, green chillies and onion.

3. After cooking this mixture for 5 minutes, add the ginger and garlic. Gently stir while cooking for a further 3 minutes.

4. Add the ground turmeric, salt, sugar and mashed potatoes to the pan. Thoroughly mix all the ingredients together. Taste the mixture to check that the salt levels are to your liking.

5. Add some water, a little at a time, to help loosen the aloo bhaji. Keep the pan on a low heat for a few minutes, then turn off the heat and place a lid on the pan until you are ready to serve. To reheat, simply add a little boiling water to help loosen the mixture once again.

6. If you like, scatter the aloo bhaji with fresh coriander just before serving.

Notes: If you are going to incorporate this spiced potato mixture into samosas, paratha, dosa or bonda, it is best to work with it once it has cooled slightly.

Appam

**Preparation time: 20 minutes +
2-4 hours resting
Cooking time: 3-4 minutes per appam
Makes 7**

5g easy-bake dried active yeast

1 tbsp white sugar

50ml lukewarm water

350g rice flour

1 x 400ml tin of full-fat coconut milk

50ml warm water

½ tsp salt

One of many joys of spending time in Kerala, and indeed Sri Lanka, is the breakfast offering of appam. In Sri Lanka they are referred to as hoppers. These crisp, bowl-shaped rice pancakes are served at breakfast, often with an egg in the centre and some chutney on the side along with some dal or sambar. It really is a wonderful way to start your day. Back in the UK, I tend to make mine for lunch as they are quite substantial. They would also be great for a weekend brunch.

1. Place the yeast, sugar and lukewarm water into a bowl, give the mixture a stir and then set aside for 15 minutes.

2. In a larger bowl, combine the rice flour and coconut milk. Pour in the yeast mixture once it has frothed and therefore activated. Stir well so the batter is smooth and thick. Add some of the warm water to loosen until it's the same consistency as pancake batter.

3. If you live in a warm climate, you can leave the bowl in the sun, covered with a clean tea towel. If you live in a colder climate, put the bowl in a switched off oven with the pilot light left on. Leave for 2-4 hours, allowing the batter to froth on the top.

4. When ready to make your appam, add the salt and give the batter another good stir. When you pour a ladleful back in the bowl, it should flow easily without seeming too runny or too thick. You can add more water or rice flour at this stage if needed.

5. Heat an appam pan over a medium heat (too hot and the batter will split and not stick to the sides of the pan). If you are using a non-stick appam pan, you do not need to add any oil. Otherwise, put a little oil on some kitchen roll and grease the pan before cooking each one.

6. Place one ladleful of batter into the centre of the pan. Use both hands to hold the pan and gently swirl the mixture around the edge so that it almost reaches the top. Place on a medium-low heat and keep the temperature constant.

7. If you are going to make egg appam, crack an egg into the centre of the pan and place a lid on. Cook for 3-4 minutes so that the sides of the appam begin to crisp up and the egg is cooked sufficiently. If you haven't added an egg, cook the appam in just the same way.

8. If you are using a non-stick pan, the appam will easily slide onto a plate. If not, loosen with a sharp knife to help it out of the pan.

9. Serve immediately with some Sri Lankan dal (see page 85) or sambar (see page 86) and Sri Lankan onion sambol (see page 191).

Dosas Two Ways

**Preparation time: minimum 4 hours
for Green Goddess Dosa
20 minutes for Rava Dosa
Cooking time: 2-3 minutes per dosa
Makes 6-7**

For the rava dosa

180g fine semolina

125g plain yoghurt

300ml cold water

1 tsp salt, or to taste

½ tsp caster sugar

½ tsp baking powder

For the green goddess dosa

200g green moong/mung lentils

50g fresh spinach

1-2 fresh green chillies

2.5cm (1 inch) fresh ginger, finely
grated

1 tsp salt

100g rice flour

300ml water

For both dosa

1 tsp vegetable oil or ghee per dosa

Dosas are thin savoury crepes eaten for breakfast or lunch in South India, typically made from fermented rice and urid dal. Mine are speedy versions which forgo hours of fermenting, so are not strictly authentic but provide easy alternatives. Back in the UK I eat them at lunch time, often stuffed with my aloo bhaji recipe (see page 32). These two versions are straightforward to make, although one requires a minimum of 4 hours soaking, and both should be the same consistency as normal pancake batter once you blitz them.

For the rava dosa

1. Mix the semolina and yoghurt together and then slowly add 200ml of the cold water until the mixture is the consistency of a thick pancake batter. Leave it to rest for 15 minutes.

2. After resting, give the mixture a good stir and add the rest of the water so that you have a super smooth and thin pancake batter consistency.

3. Add the salt, sugar and baking powder to the batter, then follow Steps 4-6 below to cook the dosa.

For the green goddess dosa

1. Soak the green moong lentils in a bowl of water for a minimum of 4 hours or overnight.

2. Once soaked, strain the lentils, place them into a blender and add the spinach, chillies, ginger and salt. Blitz to combine.

3. Add the rice flour and blend the mixture again, then gradually add the water until you have a pancake batter consistency. Follow Steps 4-6 below to cook the dosa.

For both dosa

4. Heat a non-stick tawa or large frying pan. Pour a drop of oil in and use some kitchen roll to wipe it around the pan. When the pan is hot enough, it will sizzle when you flick a little water into it. Pour just under a full ladle of batter into the middle of the pan and use the bottom of the ladle to make a circular motion so that the batter spreads out in a wide circle.

5. Let the dosa begin to bronze and crisp up. After a minute or so, pour the oil or ghee around the dosa and a little in the middle. Then gently lift one side and fold it over so the dosa is folded in half. You can also flip the whole dosa over if you want to crisp up the upper side too (similar to what you might do with a crepe or pancake).

6. When cooked and folded to your liking, gently lift the dosa out of the pan and serve. Repeat the steps above with the remaining batter.

Notes: If you are adding my aloo bhaji to the dosa (see page 32) this should be spooned on before folding. Another idea is to eat them with a poached or fried egg on top and a spicy chutney.

Indian Eggy Bread

Preparation time: 10 minutes
Cooking time: 12-15 minutes
Serves 4

5 eggs, whisked

25ml milk

½ red onion, finely diced

2 fresh green chillies, finely diced

2 tbsp finely chopped fresh coriander, stalks included

1 tsp finely grated fresh ginger or ginger paste

1 tsp salt, or to taste

6 slices of white bread, halved

2 tbsp vegetable or rapeseed oil

I grew up eating eggy bread, or French toast as it's also known, for breakfast sometimes. I rarely had the sweet version with bacon and maple syrup, instead opting for white bread dunked into a simple egg mixture with salt and pepper, then frying it. I would then have a dollop of good old-fashioned tomato ketchup to accompany it. This version has been pimped up with a spicy kick and is hugely popular in India as well as at my house.

1. In a mixing bowl, combine all the ingredients except the bread and oil and whisk until everything is well incorporated.

2. Lay one of the slices of bread into the bowl and dunk it under the mixture, then use a spatula to turn it over.

3. Heat some of the oil in a pan and when hot, bring the bowl with the soaked bread to the pan and transfer it over gently. If you are using a large frying pan you can normally cook two slices at the same time.

4. Leave the eggy bread to bronze on one side for a couple of minutes before turning it over. Once both sides are nicely bronzed, remove and continue with the rest of the slices.

5. This is best eaten immediately when the slices are piping hot. Serve with any of the chutneys in this book that take your fancy; they'll all taste delicious with Indian eggy bread.

Indian Style Scrambled Eggs

Preparation time: 2 minutes
Cooking time: 8-9 minutes
Serves 2

2 tbsp vegetable or rapeseed oil

½ small red onion, finely diced

1 fresh green chilli, finely sliced (optional)

2 medium tomatoes, finely diced

¼ tsp ground turmeric

¼ tsp Kashmiri chilli powder (less if using a different chilli powder)

5 eggs, whisked

½ tsp salt, or to taste

Handful of fresh coriander, finely chopped including the stalks

1 tsp butter (optional)

Elevate your scrambled eggs by giving them an Indian twist that will have you hooked from the first spoonful. The trick is not to overcook the eggs; fold them gently with a spatula and keep the heat low once the eggs are in the pan. They work well with regular toast but are great with any fresh or leftover naan.

1. Heat the oil in a frying pan and when hot, add the onion and green chilli. Keep the pan on a medium heat at this stage.

2. After 3-4 minutes, add the tomatoes and cook for a further 2 minutes so they begin to soften. Stir in the ground turmeric and Kashmiri chilli powder until well mixed.

3. Add the whisked eggs and turn the heat down slightly. They should be cooked within 2.5 minutes. Immediately begin to fold the eggs with a spatula so that none get stuck on the bottom of the pan.

4. Add the salt and fresh coriander. As the eggs begin to come together, take the pan off the heat and continue to fold them. Add a dollop of butter if you are feeling extra decadent. The heat from the pan will continue to cook the eggs, but if they remain runny, place it back on the heat for an extra 10-20 seconds.

5. Serve with a steaming cup of my masala chai (see page 198).

Notes: I find the trick is to remove the pan from the heat just before the eggs are fully scrambled. When folded, they will become the right consistency.

Upma

Preparation time: 10 minutes
Cooking time: 15 minutes
Serves 4

2 tbsp vegetable oil

1 tsp black or brown mustard seeds

¼ tsp asafoetida powder

10-15 curry leaves

1-2 fresh green chillies, finely chopped (optional)

1 small red onion, finely chopped

1 heaped tsp finely grated fresh ginger or ginger paste

¼ tsp ground turmeric

1 carrot, finely diced

60g fine green beans, finely chopped

40g red peanuts or cashews

1 tsp salt, or to taste

650ml boiling water

200g coarse semolina

Fresh coriander, to garnish (optional)

This South Indian breakfast snack is simple and delicious: a family favourite in my household. Growing up, I never particularly liked semolina which was typically served in British schools as a sweet dessert, often with a dollop of jam. The Indian version is savoury, super flavoursome and a good way to include vegetables in your diet. I tend to use carrots and fine green beans but other vegetables that need using up will also work well, or you can simply add frozen peas.

1. Heat the vegetable oil in a pan on a low heat. When hot, add the mustard seeds, asafoetida, curry leaves, and chillies if using. The mustard seeds will begin to splutter immediately so be careful.

2. Add the onion and move everything around the pan to soften for the next 3-4 minutes, before adding the ginger and ground turmeric. Give the mixture a good stir.

3. Add the carrot, beans, nuts and salt and move everything around the pan for a minute before adding the boiling water. Let it simmer gently for 5 minutes, allowing the vegetables to soften, before adding the semolina, a tablespoon at a time so that lumps do not form. The mixture will then become quite thick in consistency.

4. Turn the heat down, cover the pan with a lid and allow to steam for a further 2-3 minutes. After this time, remove the pan from the heat.

5. Before serving, fluff the semolina with a fork to loosen it up and then serve with some chopped coriander if you like. You can also place the upma into an oiled ramekin before turning it out onto a plate to make it look neater if you wish.

SNACKS AND SALADS

Street food has been an established part of Indian cuisine forever and when it comes to the standard of street food, India triumphs. There is huge precision and expertise amongst the vendors, or 'wallahs' as they are called there. Each has a narrow repertoire with skills honed to perfection. You will see long queues as regulars return time after time. When I'm in Kolkata I often like to explore on foot, so stopping every now and again for a little snack breaks up the day nicely. As a rule, the street food is cooked fresh and served piping hot. Even the masala chai I adore is boiled to within an inch of its life. This is good for food hygiene and locals are very discerning in this regard. In their homes, relatives always shower us with tasty treats. You can imagine that visiting more than a couple of households in a day can entail marathon snacking!

Crispy Cumin Potatoes

Preparation time: 5 minutes
Cooking time: 15 minutes
Serves 2

2 large potatoes, peeled and cut into 2cm cubes

2 tbsp vegetable or rapeseed oil

1 tsp cumin seeds

1 fresh green chilli, finely sliced or 1 small dried red chilli (optional)

½ tsp ground turmeric

½ tsp salt, or to taste

1 small handful of fresh coriander per serving

Dollop of yoghurt per serving

½ lemon, cut into wedges

This quick and easy dish was my go-to when I felt peckish at university. It took no time to rustle up and I always had the ingredients to hand. It really hit the spot with minimal effort, served in a bowl with a dollop of yoghurt and some fresh coriander. It's also great for late night munchies.

1. Begin by parboiling the potatoes in a pan of water. This will take around 5 minutes, as they need to hold their shape and not become mushy. Drain and set aside.

2. Heat the oil in a medium-size pan with a lid. When hot, add the cumin seeds and chilli if using, and allow them to sizzle in the pan for 20 seconds.

3. Pour the parboiled potatoes into the pan and cover with the cumin seeds. Add the ground turmeric, which will turn them a vibrant yellow colour. Keep the heat low and allow the potatoes to begin to bronze and crisp up.

4. Cover with the lid, which will add moisture and allow them to soften quicker. Check after 5 minutes and leave for another 5 as required, until they have softened and are ready to eat.

5. Add the salt and stir in well. Taste, then spoon into a bowl and scatter with fresh coriander. Add a dollop of yoghurt and a squeeze of lemon juice to each bowl.

Fried White Poppy Seed Aubergine

Preparation time: 10 minutes
Cooking time: 15 minutes
Serves 4

100g gram/chickpea flour

100ml water

½ tsp ground turmeric

½ tsp Kashmiri chilli powder or dried chilli flakes (optional)

1 tsp salt, or to taste

2 tbsp white poppy seeds

4 tbsp vegetable oil per batch

1 large aubergine, sliced into 1cm thick rounds

In Bengal, these tasty aubergine pieces are known as begun bhaja and often accompany rice and dal at the beginning of a meal. It is best to serve them immediately after cooking so they are deliciously hot. You can make them simply with turmeric, chilli powder and salt, but the white poppy seed version here, known as posto diye begun bhaja, is the one I often gravitate towards.

1. First, make the batter. Combine the flour and water in a mixing bowl, aiming for a slightly thinner consistency than pancake batter. Add a little more flour or water if the batter is too thin or thick respectively, then stir in the ground turmeric, chilli and salt and mix well.

2. Set out the bowl of batter, a small bowl containing the poppy seeds and a large plate lined with kitchen roll on your work surface.

3. Heat the first 4 tablespoons of oil in a pan while you dip an aubergine round in the bowl of batter. Use your hand to cover it completely; enjoy the messy moment! Next use your fingers, or a teaspoon, to sprinkle some of the white poppy seeds on both sides of the aubergine, then place it straight into the hot oil in the pan.

4. Repeat this process to fry the aubergine in batches until both sides have lightly bronzed and crisped up. This will take around 2 minutes on each side. Place the fried aubergine on the lined plate, adding a sprinkle of salt as required, while you cook the rest.

5. Serve immediately. They are great as a snack with some masala chai or with rice and dal at the beginning of a meal.

Daler Bora - Lentil Fritters

**Preparation time: 5 minutes
+ 2 hours soaking
Cooking time: 15 minutes
Serves 4**

350g red split lentils/masoor dal, soaked in water for 2 hours

Handful of fresh coriander

1 medium-size onion, chopped

1-2 fresh green chillies, finely chopped (optional)

1 tsp salt, or to taste

1 tsp ground turmeric

Vegetable oil, for frying

Large pinch of chaat masala powder, to serve

Just as the afternoon light begins to fade, the daler bora wallah begins to prepare his offering to passers-by. He is based at the top of Park Street, near the metro, in the hot bustling metropolis of Kolkata. Each afternoon, returning to our hotel, we would pick up some of his lentil fritters. In many he stuffs some green chilli, but you can omit this part and instead have a couple blended into the dal mixture. They are best eaten piping hot with a sprinkling of chaat masala.

1. Drain the soaked lentils and place them in a blender along with the coriander, onion, chillies if using, salt and turmeric. Blitz to form a smooth, thick paste.

2. Place a small deep pan on the heat and pour in enough oil so the daler bora can float. Wait for it to reach the right temperature; test this by dropping a little of the lentil paste into the pan, and if it fizzles and rises to the top then the oil is ready.

3. Heap a teaspoon with the fritter mixture and use another to gently push it into the oil. I usually fry one first and taste it to check the chilli and salt levels, then add more if needed.

4. Place around 10 heaped teaspoons of batter into the pan and then allow them to bronze. If the oil is at the right heat, they should be done in 1-2 minutes. Turn them over halfway through with a slotted spoon.

5. Once bronzed, remove with the slotted spoon and place on kitchen roll to drain. Eat the daler bora while still hot, sprinkled with chaat masala or dipped into my coriander, mint and lime chutney (see page 192).

Red Onion Pakora

**Preparation time: 15 minutes
Cooking time: 20 minutes
Makes around 15**

150g chickpea/gram flour

½ tsp baking powder

½ tsp fenugreek seeds (optional)

1 tsp cumin seeds

1 tsp ground coriander

1 tsp salt, or to taste

2 fresh green chillies, finely sliced (leave the seeds in for more heat)

300g red onion, finely sliced

Vegetable or sunflower oil

Notes: You can also make pakora by replacing the red onions with cauliflower, mushrooms or spinach.

These crispy snacks are a common street food throughout India. They are a firm favourite at my Indian cooking classes too; we often eat them while we are waiting for the curries to finish cooking. They are addictively good and perfect pre-dinner snackage.

1. Mix everything except the red onion and oil together in a large bowl. Add a little cold water to form a thick batter, similar to a pancake batter in consistency, then stir in the finely sliced red onions so that they are fully coated.

2. Half fill a small pan with oil and heat gradually for around 6 minutes. To check the temperature, dip a few strands of batter-coated red onion into the oil. If it is ready, the oil will fizzle and if you drop the onion in, it will rise to the top.

3. Heap a teaspoon with the pakora mixture and use another to gently push it into the oil. Do not touch it at this stage. The pakora should rise to the surface and crisp up fairly quickly. I tend make about 4 at a time.

4. Leave them to fry for 2 minutes, then turn over and leave for a further 2 minutes. Once the pakora has bronzed on both sides, remove it from the pan with a slotted spoon and place on kitchen roll to soak up any excess oil.

5. Try one pakora before continuing so you can check it is cooked through and has the right salt and chilli levels for you, then adjust the batter accordingly.

6. Serve hot and dip into any of the smooth chutneys (see page 184).

Dhokla

Preparation time: 20 minutes
Cooking time: 10-12 minutes
Makes about 26 small pieces (I use a 20cm/8 inch cake tin)

200 gram/chickpea flour

I tsp caster sugar

I tsp salt, or to taste

¼ tsp ground turmeric

¼ tsp asafoetida powder

I tbsp lemon juice

I tsp Eno fruit salt

For the tempering

2 tbsp vegetable or rapeseed oil

I tsp black or brown mustard seeds

2-4 fresh green chillies, sliced lengthways

10-15 curry leaves

125ml water

I tsp caster sugar

I tsp salt

I tbsp lemon juice

This Gujarati savoury steamed sponge cake is made of gram flour and is a favourite of mine. On my spice tours we stop for snacks at a local Asian bakery, and I always get my clients to try dhokla. It's moist and gluten-free and is delicious with black or brown mustard seeds, curry leaves and green chillies on top. It certainly makes a lovely tea-time treat with a mug of hot masala chai. Eno fruit salt, which is a crucial component of this recipe, is something you can easily pick up at any pharmacy.

1. Mix the flour with the caster sugar, salt, ground turmeric and asafoetida powder in a large bowl. Stir in the lemon juice and enough cold water to bring the consistency to that of pancake batter, adding just a little at a time.

2. Use a handheld whisk to really bring the mixture together and then leave it to rest for 10 minutes. Give the rested batter another mix, then fold in the Eno fruit salt. This is what will give the dhokla air and lightness.

3. Meanwhile, grease a 20cm (8 inch) cake tin with a little oil and place a pan of water with a lid on a medium heat. Place a round biscuit cutter or a steamer rack into the pan and place the tin on top of this, so that it sits above the water.

4. Pour the dhokla batter carefully into the cake tin and then place the lid on the pan. Keep the water at a gently rolling boil for 10 minutes.

5. While the dhokla is steaming, prepare the tempering ingredients. Heat the oil in a small pan and then add the mustard seeds, green chillies and curry leaves.

6. Add the water to the tempering pan followed by the sugar, salt and lemon juice. Allow to simmer for a couple of minutes, then set aside.

7. Returning to the dhokla, use a sharp knife or toothpick to make a small incision in the top of the sponge. If the knife comes out clean, it is ready. If not, allow it to steam for a few more minutes.

8. Carefully remove the cake tin from the pan and allow to cool slightly before gently placing a plate on top of cake tin and turning it over, allowing the dhokla to come out.

9. Gently cut the dhokla into bite-size squares and then gently spoon the sweet, salty, sour, hot tempering mixture on top of the dhokla. You may not need to add all the liquid, but make sure the spices are evenly scattered on top.

Kachumber Salad

Preparation time: 15 minutes
Serves 4

1 medium-size cucumber

4 medium tomatoes

1 small red onion

1 fresh green or red chilli (optional)

Handful of fresh coriander

½ lemon or lime

Salt and pepper, to taste

No Indian feast is complete without a kachumber salad. Its simplicity and cooling notes work in harmony with curries, cutting through the spice with fresh, crunchy textures. The only preparation is cutting a handful of vegetables with neatness and precision. It's also a perfect accompaniment to barbecue banquets on hot summer days.

1. First, peel the cucumber in alternate strips and cut it lengthways down the middle, then scoop out the seeds with a teaspoon. Cut each half lengthways again and then cut into 1cm cubes and place in a mixing bowl. Dice the tomatoes into similar-size cubes and add these to the bowl.

2. Chop the red onion a little more finely than the cucumber and tomato, then add to the bowl. If you want to give the salad a little kick, finely slice the chilli and add it to the mixing bowl. Leave the seeds in for more heat, or use a smaller amount, it's totally up to you.

3. Finely chop the fresh coriander, using the leaves and stalks. Stalks add a huge amount of flavour so don't discard them. Add both to the mixing bowl.

4. Squeeze the lemon or lime juice over the salad and gently fold everything together. Add more juice if you like, to create the right balance of sour notes.

5. Season the salad with salt and pepper to taste, then transfer it to a serving bowl.

Sweet Potato Tikki

Preparation time: 45 minutes
Cooking time: approx. 1 hour
Makes 12

4 large sweet potatoes, skin on

5-6 tbsp fine golden breadcrumbs

3 tbsp rice flour or cornflour

1 tsp finely grated fresh ginger or ginger paste

1 tsp chaat masala powder

1 tsp salt, or to taste

½ tsp red chilli flakes

½ tsp Kashmiri chilli powder (less if you are using a different chilli powder)

Handful of fresh coriander, chopped

3 tbsp vegetable or rapeseed oil

Aloo tikki are fritters often made with white potatoes, but I like to replace these with sweet potatoes. They are the perfect savoury afternoon treat when friends come round, accompanied by a chutney and a steaming cup of masala chai, but particularly moreish so be sure to make a big batch!

1. Using a fork, prick the sweet potatoes and place them on a baking tray in a preheated oven at 200°C/180°C Fan/400°F/Gas Mark 6 for 40-50 minutes, or until the flesh is soft when poked with a sharp knife.

2. Peel the roasted sweet potatoes, then mash the flesh in a mixing bowl. Add all the remaining ingredients except the oil. Stir the tikki mixture well, then taste test to check you have the right balance of salty, hot and sour notes. Depending on the size of the sweet potatoes, you may need to add more breadcrumbs. The texture you are aiming for is a firm mashed potato.

4. Use your hands to roll the mixture into golf balls and then flatten these slightly. Place on a plate, cover and leave in the fridge for 30 minutes to firm up.

5. Warm the oil in a frying pan on a medium heat. When hot, add the tikki in batches so that they bronze nicely. This should take around 3 minutes on each side. Do not move them around the pan or they will break up. Wait for them to bronze before carefully turning them over. Transfer the first batch to a plate lined with kitchen paper while you cook the rest.

6. Serve the tikki hot and eat just as they are, or with either a tamarind and date chutney (see page 192) or a coriander and mint chutney (see page 192).

Indian Savoury Doughnuts

Preparation time: minimum 4 hours soaking + 15 minutes
Cooking time: 20 minutes
Makes 15

250g urid dal (also known as skinned black gram)

40-50ml cold water

1 small red onion, chopped

2 tsp finely chopped or grated fresh ginger

2 fresh green chillies, finely chopped (optional)

10-15 curry leaves, chopped (optional)

1 tsp salt, or to taste

3-5 tbsp rice flour, as required

Vegetable or sunflower oil, for frying

These South Indian snacks, known as medu vada, are commonly eaten at breakfast. They are made mainly from the white urid dal, which are black lentils that have been split and skinned. Soaking for a few hours is required, but then they are straightforward to make. The shaping and transferring into the pan of hot oil does take patience and practice, but once you have got a handle on them, they are great fun to make and eat. Typically, I serve these as a snack with some chutney when friends come over for supper.

1. Put the urid dal in a bowl, cover with water and leave to soak for a minimum of 4 hours. Drain the soaked dal completely, then place into a blender and blitz briefly. Gradually add the cold water to help the mixture become smooth but not too wet in consistency.

2. Add the onion, ginger, chillies, curry leaves and salt to the dal in the blender and blitz until smooth. Add the rice flour gradually to help thicken the mixture and blitz again. The dough should be thick enough to be scooped up with your hand and shaped into a ball.

3. Half-fill a small pan with oil, so that you don't need to use so much, and heat until a little bit of batter dropped into the oil rises to the surface immediately and begins to fizzle.

4. Wet one of your hands, scoop out a golf ball-sized piece of the dough and make a hole in the centre with your finger to create a doughnut shape.

5. Gently loosen the dough and slide it gently off your finger into the hot oil. Try to lower the doughnut into the pan and remove your hand smoothly and quickly, taking care as you do. The more you make, the more you'll get the hang of this motion.

6. Place a few doughnuts in the pan at once and leave them to bronze on one side for 2-3 minutes before turning them over with a slotted spoon to fry for another couple of minutes. You are looking for a lightly bronzed colour (not brown) so watch them closely.

7. Remove the doughnuts from the pan with the slotted spoon and place on kitchen roll to absorb the excess oil. Once the first one has cooked and cooled enough, do a taste test and add more salt, chilli, ginger or curry leaves to the dough as you see fit. Simply blitz again if required. If you are planning to serve them as a snack when friends come over, place the cooked doughnuts in a preheated oven that has been turned off until you are ready to serve.

Notes: These are delicious dunked into a chutney. I recommend my coriander, mint and lime chutney (see page 192), date and tamarind chutney (page 192) or South Indian tomato and date chutney (page 188).

Spiced Okra Munchies

Preparation time: 15 minutes
Cooking time: 20-25 minutes
Serves 4-6

500g okra

2 tbsp vegetable or rapeseed oil

1 tsp salt, or to taste

½ tsp cayenne pepper

¼ tsp ground turmeric

You may have come across okra fries, which are deep fried in a spiced gram/chickpea flour batter. These are quite different as the okra is baked in the oven to crisp up, much like kale crisps. They are perfect with a cold beer or glass of wine. I've fed them to friends who were new to the delights of okra, and they couldn't get over how deliciously moreish they were.

1. Wash and dry the okra thoroughly, then trim off the ends and chop the okra into 1-2cm pieces. Meanwhile, preheat the oven to 240°C/220°C Fan/475°F/Gas Mark 9.

2. Place the prepared okra in a bowl with all the other ingredients, then use your hands to mix everything together.

3. Scatter the spiced okra evenly over the baking tray. Place in the hot oven for 20-25 minutes until they are crispy. The okra will also massively reduce in size.

4. Transfer the okra munchies to a small bowl, sprinkle with a little more salt if necessary and eat immediately. Serve with tamarind and date chutney (see page 192).

Tuna Fish Bora

Preparation time: 25 minutes
Cooking time: 10-15 minutes
Makes 10

370g potatoes

½ small red onion, finely chopped

1 fresh green chilli, very finely chopped

2 tbsp finely chopped fresh coriander (use the leaves and stalks)

1 heaped tsp finely grated fresh ginger or ginger paste

1 tsp ground cumin

1 tsp salt, or to taste

1 x 145g tin of tuna, drained completely

1 egg, whisked

50g panko breadcrumbs

4 tbsp vegetable or rapeseed oil

In Bengal, fish bora are known as 'macher bora' and these little snacks are always a welcome treat either to have on their own, with a chutney, or as part of a meal such as the cherry tomato masoor dal (see page 70) and rice. You can use whatever fish you have to hand, cooked and then flaked. We tend to make these with tinned tuna, which works well and is easily available.

1. Boil the potatoes in their skins for 10-15 minutes until soft. Pierce with a fork to check they are done, then drain and leave to cool. Peel and mash the cooled potatoes.

2. In a bowl, combine the red onion, green chilli, fresh coriander, ginger, ground cumin and salt, using your fingers to mix it all together well.

3. Add the tuna to the bowl and mix in well so that everything is combined, then stir in the mashed potato. Taste a little of the mixture to check the salt levels, adding more if needed. If you'd like it hotter, add another finely chopped chilli.

4. Using your hands, shape the mixture into golf balls and lightly press down to flatten slightly. Place all the bora on a plate, put the whisked egg in a bowl and the breadcrumbs in another.

5. Heat the oil in a frying pan. Dip one of the bora into the egg, then the breadcrumbs, then straight into the pan. Do this in batches so as not to overcrowd the pan.

6. Keep the pan on a medium heat and the patties will bronze quickly. Check them after a minute and if they are ready, turn them over to cook for another minute. Turn them on their sides so that the whole of the patty is sufficiently bronzed before transferring to a plate lined with kitchen roll. Keep the cooked patties in a warm oven while you fry the rest.

7. Serve the tuna bora hot; they are great on their own or dipped into a tamarind and date chutney (see page 192).

Chaat Salad

Preparation time: 15 minutes
Cooking time: 10 minutes
Serves 4-6

This salad has elements of the tasty Indian street food snacks papri chaat and bhel puri. The key ingredient here is a spice mix called chaat masala, which includes dry mango, black salt, cumin, pomegranate seeds, coriander, mint, ginger, asafoetida and cloves. The overall taste is a mix of zingy, sour, sweet and salty flavours. When I visit India, I always try to eat from a number of papri chaat and bhel puri wallahs, each with their own unique recipe.

2 large potatoes, unpeeled

3 large tomatoes, diced

½ cucumber, peeled and deseeded then cut into half moons

1 small red onion, finely diced

1 large handful of fresh coriander, chopped

1 fresh green chilli, finely sliced or 1 tsp chilli flakes (optional)

1 tbsp vegetable or rapeseed oil

1 tsp black or brown mustard seeds

1 x 400g tin or jar of chickpeas, drained

1 tsp salt, or to taste

½ lemon or lime, juice only

2 tsp chaat masala powder

2 tbsp either boondi, sev or Bombay mix

2 tbsp fresh pomegranate seeds, to serve (optional)

1. Boil the potatoes in their skins until soft. Use a fork to check they have softened enough, then drain and leave to cool. Peel the skins off the cooled potatoes and dice into 2cm cubes.

2. Meanwhile, prepare the tomatoes, cucumber, red onion, fresh coriander and green chilli if using. Mix them all together in a large bowl.

3. Heat the oil in a pan and then add the mustard seeds. They will begin to splutter so be careful when cooking with them. After 15 seconds, add the drained chickpeas and coat them in the oil and mustard seeds, moving them around the pan for a minute.

4. Remove the pan from the heat and pour the contents into a bowl. Once the chickpea mixture has cooled, combine it with the salad in the large bowl and the diced potatoes.

5. Add the salt, lemon or lime juice and chaat masala powder to the salad and mix into the other ingredients. The chaat masala powder is integral to this recipe and is found in most large supermarkets or Asian grocers and online: see my spice suppliers section on page 228.

6. Stir in the boondi, sev or Bombay mix just before serving or it will become soggy. Finally, scatter the fresh pomegranate seeds on top and serve at room temperature. This salad works well alongside a barbecue. In India, they always put a little tamarind chutney on top and sometimes some natural yoghurt, but it's up to you. If you want to add some, try my tamarind and date chutney on page 192.

Notes: If you can find them, either boondi (salted fried chickpea flour puffs), sev (fried chickpea noodles) or Bombay mix will add crunch and more texture to the salad. Alternatively, you can substitute these with crushed tortilla chips.

Chicken Kathi Rolls

Preparation time: 45 minutes + 30 minutes marinating
Cooking time: 40-50 minutes
Makes 6

For the marinated chicken

600g boneless and skinless chicken thighs or breasts, cut into bite-size pieces

3 tbsp plain yoghurt

2 tbsp ginger-garlic paste (see page 220)

1 tbsp vegetable or rapeseed oil

2 tsp tandoori masala powder

1 tsp Kashmiri chilli powder (less if using a different chilli powder)

1 tsp each ground cumin, coriander and garam masala

½ tsp freshly ground black pepper

½ tsp salt, or to taste

For the rolls and filling

1 batch of paratha (see page 180)

1 batch of coriander, mint and lime chutney (see page 192)

1 large red onion

1 lemon, juiced

½ cucumber

2 tbsp vegetable or rapeseed oil

2 medium white onions, finely sliced

½ tsp Kashmiri chilli powder (less if using a different chilli powder)

½ tsp each ground cumin, coriander and garam masala

6 eggs, whisked

2 tsp chaat masala powder

Kathi rolls are Kolkata's answer to a Lebanese wrap. They are made of flaky paratha smothered in ghee and egg, with the addition of either paneer, chicken or lamb. Kathi comes from the Bengali word meaning stick, referring to how they were originally made using bamboo skewers to roast the meat. Raw onion and cucumber are often added for extra bite and texture, along with a chilli sauce. Kusums and Nizams are the places to go for one if you are in Kolkata; Nizams were reputedly the founder of this culinary creation back in the 1930s.

1. For the marinated chicken, place all the ingredients into a bowl and mix well so that the chicken is coated in the spiced yoghurt. Cover and leave to marinate in the fridge for 30 minutes. If you are using wooden skewers, place them in cold water to soak now, so they don't burn when you put them in the oven.

2. While the chicken is marinating, prepare the dough for the paratha and make the coriander, mint and lime chutney.

3. Preheat the oven to 200°C/180°C Fan/400°F/Gas Mark 6. Thread a few pieces of chicken onto each of the soaked bamboo skewers or use metal ones. Place them in the preheated oven to cook for 20 minutes, turning twice during this time so that they are cooked evenly.

4. While the chicken is cooking, start preparing the filling. Finely slice the red onion and halve the cucumber lengthways, then cut into half moons. Heat the oil in a pan and add the sliced white onions. Cook on a medium-low heat for the next 6-8 minutes until lightly bronzed and then add the Kashmiri chilli powder and the ground cumin, coriander and garam masala.

5. Remove the chicken from the oven after 20 minutes and slide the meat off the skewers. Add it to the spiced onion to finish cooking for 5 minutes.

6. Cook the paratha according to the recipe, then heat a frying pan and add a large spoonful of the whisked egg to the pan. Place the first cooked paratha on top so it sticks to the egg layer. Leave the egg to cook for a minute, then remove from the pan and start on the next paratha with another spoonful of egg. You should have enough to make 6 rolls.

7. To fill the kathi rolls, spoon the chicken and onion mixture onto the eggy side of the paratha in a line down the centre. Add some raw red onion, lemon juice and cucumber followed by the fresh coriander, mint and lime chutney. Sprinkle a little chaat masala down the centre and then wrap up like a tortilla.

8. Repeat with the remaining paratha and filling. The kathi rolls are best eaten straight away, while they are still hot.

Notes: To make a vegetarian kathi roll, simply replace the chicken with paneer. If preferred, you can soften the finely sliced raw red onion by placing it in a jam jar and covering with equal amounts of rice wine, white, red or cider vinegar and warm water. Add a teaspoon of salt, then leave for 10 minutes after which time the onions will have turned a vivid pink and softened nicely.

DALS AND SOUPS

I can't think of anything more comforting than a warming bowl of dal on a cold winter's evening. It is equally uplifting in the summer months when a bowl of dal hits the spot for a light lunch or supper. There are so many varieties, each tasting completely different, so I hope that everyone finds at least one dal to suit their own tastes. They are super nutritious, healthy, affordable and straightforward to make. You will also find a few delicious soups, which are thinner in consistency than most of the dals, but still pack in plenty of flavour.

Dhaba Style Dal Fry

Preparation time: 10 minutes + 30-60 minutes soaking
Cooking time: 50-60 minutes
Serves 6

250g plain toor dal

150g yellow moong/mung dal

1.3 litres water

2 tbsp vegetable or rapeseed oil

1 tsp cumin seeds

2 dried red chillies, broken in half

Pinch of asafoetida powder

8 curry leaves (optional)

1 red onion, finely chopped

1 tsp salt, or to taste

1 tsp finely grated fresh ginger or ginger paste

1 tsp finely grated garlic or garlic paste

1 tsp ground turmeric

½ tsp ground cumin

½ tsp ground coriander

½ tsp ground garam masala

2 tomatoes, finely diced

2 tbsp finely chopped fresh coriander

1 tbsp ghee or oil

3 cloves of garlic, finely sliced

This dal is found in roadside cafes, or dhaba, in India, especially along highways and at truck stops and petrol stations. Don't underestimate the quality of food served, though. I have had some truly memorable meals in India at these very basic pitstops where homestyle local cooking can be witnessed and tasted. You will notice that two different types of lentil are required in this dal.

1. If you have time, soak the dals in a bowl covered with water for up to an hour before cooking. Typically, I miss this part out and instead place both dals in a pan, cover them with water and gently boil for 45 minutes until they are soft when pinched between your thumb and forefinger. Scum will form on the surface while they cook, so remove it with a large spoon and discard as needed.

2. While the dal is boiling, prepare the tempering ingredients. Begin by heating the oil in a large non-stick pan. When hot, add the cumin seeds, dried chillies, asafoetida and curry leaves.

3. After 20 seconds, add the red onion and salt and cook for 5 minutes so that the onion softens. Stir in the ginger and garlic followed by the ground turmeric, cumin, coriander and garam masala.

4. After 2 minutes, add the tomatoes and allow them to soften, which will take another couple of minutes. Fold half the fresh coriander into the tomato and onion mixture.

5. Once the dal has softened completely, use a potato masher to roughly mash it so that it becomes smoother.

6. Put 2 large serving spoons of the dal into the pan with the spiced tomato and onion mixture. Move it around the pan and then return the contents to the main dal pan.

7. Fold the spices into the dal and leave it to cook on a low heat for a further 5 minutes. You can add more water if you prefer a more soup-like consistency, which I often do. Check the salt level and add more if necessary.

8. Before serving the dal, heat a small pan and add the ghee or oil. When hot, add the thinly sliced garlic and stir until it begins to bronze, watching carefully as it can burn fast.

9. Finally, pour the ghee and garlic into the dal, stir in and scatter with the remaining fresh coriander to serve.

Black-Eyed Beans with Tamarind and Coconut

Preparation time: 15 minutes
Cooking time: 30 minutes
Serves 4-6

45g tamarind pulp (from a block) or 1-2 tsp tamarind concentrate paste

300ml boiling water

1 white onion, roughly chopped

3 cloves of garlic, roughly chopped

2.5cm (1 inch) fresh ginger, roughly chopped

2 tbsp vegetable or rapeseed oil

1 tsp brown or black mustard seeds

1 tsp cumin seeds

½ tsp fenugreek/methi seeds

1 tsp salt

1 tsp ground turmeric

1 tsp ground coriander

1 tsp Kashmiri chilli powder

3 large tomatoes, roughly chopped

2 x 400ml tins of black-eyed beans, drained

100ml coconut milk

Handful of fresh coriander, to serve

Black-eyed beans are a fantastic pulse that we seldom come across in Western Europe and this recipe is a great way of incorporating them into your diet. While you can use the dried variety, this recipe uses tinned black-eyed beans and therefore takes very little time to prepare which makes it ideal for a weeknight supper. It also happens to be vegan.

1. Place the tamarind pulp in a small bowl and cover with about 200ml of the boiling water. Use the back of a spoon to break up the tamarind and then leave it to soak for 15 minutes. If using tamarind concentrate paste, skip this step.

2. Meanwhile, blitz the chopped onion, garlic and ginger in a food processor until smooth.

3. Heat the oil in a deep, wide pan. When hot, add the mustard, cumin and fenugreek seeds. They will immediately begin to sizzle so be careful they don't spit or jump out of the pan.

4. Add the onion paste, salt and ground spices to the pan, mix well and turn down the heat. Cook gently for 10 minutes, stirring at intervals and adding a little more oil if required. You want the raw smell from the onion and garlic to dissipate and the paste to begin to lightly bronze.

5. Blend the tomatoes in the food processor until smooth, then add them to the pan. Simmer gently for 5 minutes and then add the black-eyed beans. Stir them into the sauce and place a lid on the pan.

6. Continue to simmer the beans while you strain the tamarind pulp, retaining the liquid and any paste that comes through the sieve. Stir this into the sauce, discarding any fibrous parts or stones from the tamarind. If using tamarind concentrate paste, add 1 teaspoon now.

7. Keep the heat low and simmer for 3 minutes before adding the coconut milk and remaining boiling water, then simmer for a further 10 minutes.

8. Taste the sauce to check the salt and sourness levels and then add the remaining tamarind concentrate paste if more sour notes are required. Sprinkle fresh coriander on top just before serving.

Coconut and Sultana Chana Dal

**Preparation time: 5 minutes +
soaking for at least 2 hours or
overnight
Cooking time: 40-50 minutes
Serves 4-6**

300g chana dal

1.6 litres cold water

2 tbsp vegetable or rapeseed oil

1 tsp panch phoron/Bengali five spice

2-3 Indian bay leaves/tej patta

1 tsp ground turmeric

½ tsp Kashmiri chilli powder (more if
you prefer it hot)

50g sultanas

1-2 tsp sugar, to taste

1 tsp salt, or to taste

100ml warm water

2-3 tbsp desiccated or freshly grated
coconut

This recipe is Bengali by origin and was taught to me in my 20s by my mother-in-law. Chana dal is also known as cholar, Bengal gram and yellow split chickpeas (do not confuse it with yellow split peas, which are completely different and cannot be used here!). This dal has delicate sweet undertones from the coconut, sultanas, and a little bit of added sugar. The thickness is totally up to you. Do not add salt to the lentils until they have softened completely at the end of the cooking process. Delicious mopped up with luchi (see page 176).

1. Before cooking, soak the chana dal in a bowl of cold water for a few hours or overnight. Make sure the lentils are fully submerged beneath the cold water. This will cut down the cooking time and make the lentils more digestible.

2. Drain the soaked lentils, transfer them to a large pan and cover with the 1.6 litres of fresh cold water. Boil on a medium-low heat so the water bubbles gently throughout. Scum will form on the surface during this process so simply remove with a spoon and discard.

3. The lentils will begin to soften after around 40-50 minutes. You will know they are soft when you are able to squeeze them easily between your forefinger and thumb. If they are still a little hard, simply boil them for a little longer. If all the water has been soaked up, add a little more.

4. Once the lentils are soft, use a potato masher to mash them to your preferred consistency. They don't all have to be mashed but mashing some gives the dal a delicious creamy texture.

5. In a large clean pan, warm the oil on a low heat. When hot, add the panch phoron, bay leaves, ground turmeric, chilli powder, sultanas, sugar and salt.

6. Move this mixture around the pan for 20 seconds so that the spices do not burn and then add the dal to the spices. Mix well, taste and add more sugar or salt if necessary. The dal should have a balanced sweet and salty flavour.

7. Add the final 100ml of water and simmer for a few minutes, adding a little more water if needed. Sprinkle the desiccated or freshly grated coconut over the top of the dal and simmer for another minute, then fold in the coconut and add more to serve if you like.

Ginger and Lemongrass Prawn Bisque

Preparation time: 10 minutes
Cooking time: 45 minutes
Serves 4-6

600g prawn shells and heads

1 red onion, roughly chopped

1 clove of garlic, roughly chopped

2.5cm (1 inch) fresh ginger, skin on, bruised

2 lemongrass stalks, ends removed, roughly chopped

1-2 dried red chillies

2 European bay leaves

8 black peppercorns

1 tsp salt

1.3 litres boiling water

1 tbsp butter

½ tsp smoked paprika

½ lime or lemon, juiced

1 tbsp tomato purée

1 tsp caster sugar

2 tsp cornflour or plain flour

5 tbsp cold water

I have included a few prawn curries in this book, so thought it would be a good idea to share my spiced prawn bisque too, which uses up the discarded prawn heads and shells. I buy my prawns with the shells and heads left on and freeze them after making prawn curry until I have time to make this, then bring them back to room temperature before starting to cook or run under cold water for 10-15 minutes to thaw fully. It's well worth the forward-planning and makes a lovely starter or light lunch.

1. Place the prawn shells and heads in a deep pan and add the red onion, garlic, ginger, lemongrass, chillies, bay leaves, black peppercorns and salt. Cover with the boiling water and bring to a gentle boil.

2. Simmer gently for 30 minutes, making sure the prawn shells and heads are submerged. Stir from time to time.

3. Use a handheld blender to blitz the contents of the pan as much as possible, then pour the mixture through a sieve into a large bowl. Discard everything left in the sieve.

4. Clean the original pan, place it back on the heat and add the butter. When it has melted, add the smoked paprika, lime or lemon juice and tomato purée. Move this mixture around the pan for 20 seconds and then pour the sieved liquid back into the pan.

5. Taste the bisque and then add the sugar and extra salt as required. In a small bowl, mix the cornflour and cold water to a smooth paste, then stir this into the bisque to help thicken it slightly. Leave to simmer for a further 10 minutes and then the bisque is ready to serve.

Cherry Tomato Masoor Dal

Preparation time: 5 minutes
Cooking time: 15 minutes
Serves 4

300g red split lentils/masoor dal

1 litre water

8 cherry tomatoes, whole or halved

1 tbsp vegetable or rapeseed oil, or ghee

1 heaped tsp panch phoron/Bengali five spice

2 fresh green chillies, halved lengthways

1 tsp ground turmeric

1 tsp salt, to taste

1 lemon, cut into wedges

Fresh coriander, to serve

Natural yoghurt, to serve

This dal is the culinary equivalent of a warming hug and is perfect when your body seeks nourishment in minimal time. I have added cherry tomatoes, but you can add any vegetable, just focus on one rather than a mix. If using a root vegetable, add them when you cover the dal with water at the beginning. If you prefer a softer vegetable such as courgette, marrow, peas or spinach, add these in the last 5 minutes.

1. Place the red split lentils in a pan, cover with water and use your hand to clean the lentils. Drain off the water and then repeat a couple of times, discarding the water each time.

2. Cover the washed lentils with 900ml of fresh water and bring to the boil on a low heat. Scum will form on the surface so use a spoon to remove and discard this.

3. If the water is soaked up before the lentils are cooked, simply add more. You won't be draining the dal so just add a little at the time, but enough to allow the dal to soften easily.

4. The lentils will change from orange to yellow in colour and will be cooked within 15 minutes. Add the cherry tomatoes once the dal has softened and has turned yellow.

5. In a small frying pan, heat the oil or ghee and then add the panch phoron, chillies and ground turmeric. Once the panch phoron begins to pop and release the flavours – this will take around 20 seconds – give it a quick stir and then pour the mixture into the dal.

6. Stir in the salt and then check whether you need to add a little more. Dal does require salt to bring out the flavours so it's important to do a taste test at this stage.

7. You can add a squeeze of lemon juice now or simply serve the lemon wedges on the side of each portion. Top the finished dal with some fresh coriander and a dollop of natural yoghurt.

Notes: If preferred, you can use dried red chillies instead of the fresh green chillies for this dal.

Green Mung, Garlic and Tomato Dal

**Preparation time: 5 minutes +
soaking overnight
Cooking time: 40 minutes
Serves 4**

200g green mung beans

700ml water

3 tbsp vegetable or rapeseed oil

2 Indian bay leaves

2 fresh green chillies, halved

1 heaped tsp finely grated fresh ginger
or ginger paste

8 cloves of garlic, peeled but whole

200g tinned tomatoes

¼ tsp Kashmiri chilli powder

½ tsp ground turmeric

1 tsp salt

Large handful of fresh coriander,
roughly chopped including stalks
(approx. 10g)

1 tsp chaat masala powder

Green mung beans, also known as moong, are hugely versatile and can be used in a salad once they have sprouted or in a dal pre-sprouting, although they do need to be soaked overnight. The following day you need to boil them for 30 minutes to soften them completely. As you can see, this recipe does require some forward planning, but it is worth it. I like to eat the dal with some plain rice and a vegetable curry on the side or sometimes a bowl on its own, as it's deliciously filling and tasty.

1. First, put the green mung beans in a bowl and cover them with cold water to several centimetres (a couple of inches) above the beans. Leave to soak overnight.

2. The next day, drain the beans and transfer them to a pan with the 700ml of fresh water. Boil gently until they are soft, which will take around 30 minutes. Top up with a little water if needed, as the beans will soak it up. They are ready when you can pinch a bean between your thumb and forefinger that is soft with no bite. Do not drain the green mung beans.

3. Heat the oil in a separate deep pan. When hot, add the Indian bay leaves, green chillies and ginger. Stir for 20 seconds, then add the softened green mung beans and any liquid that may still remain in the pan.

4. Add the garlic, tinned tomatoes, Kashmiri chilli, ground turmeric, salt and fresh coriander (including the stalks, which are packed full of flavour). Add a little more water to loosen everything and simmer gently for 15 minutes.

5. Stir the chaat masala powder into the dal. If you prefer your dal thicker, let it simmer a little longer before serving.

Notes: If you make this dal ahead of time, you will find that when it cools it will thicken slightly. Simply add a little boiling water to loosen when reheating.

Rajma – Red Kidney Bean Curry

Preparation time: 15 minutes
Cooking time: 30 minutes
Serves 4-6

2 red onions, roughly chopped

2.5cm (1 inch) fresh ginger or 2 tsp ginger paste

4 cloves of garlic or 2 tsp garlic paste

4 large tomatoes

2 tbsp vegetable or rapeseed oil

1 tsp cumin seeds

2 Indian bay leaves

3 cloves

2 small cinnamon sticks

1 black cardamom pod

1 tsp salt, or to taste

½ tsp ground turmeric

½ tsp ground cumin

½ tsp ground coriander

½ tsp ground garam masala

½ tsp Kashmiri chilli powder

2 x 400g tins of red kidney beans (480g once drained)

300ml water

1 tsp dried fenugreek leaves

1 tbsp chopped fresh coriander, to serve (optional)

Rajma means kidney bean in Hindi and this healthy and delicious curry is eaten throughout the northern states of India, particularly the Punjab. Traditionally, raw red kidney beans are soaked overnight and then softened in a pressure cooker for 20 minutes or cooked in a regular pan for around 50 minutes. I find using jarred or tinned red kidney beans more time-efficient and the result is an equally delicious vegan curry that has complexity and depth of flavour from all the spices.

1. First, blend the chopped red onions into a smooth purée. Do the same with the ginger and garlic if using fresh, or finely grate them to a paste consistency. Blend the tomatoes separately until smooth.

2. Add the oil to a medium-size, wide pan with a lid. When hot, add the cumin seeds, bay leaves, cloves, cinnamon sticks and black cardamom pod. Move them around the pan for 20 seconds and then add the onion purée.

3. Stir in the salt to help the onion soften and speed up the bronzing process. Keep the pan on a medium-low heat for 5-7 minutes, so that the raw smell dissipates and the onions begin to bronze.

4. Stir the ginger and garlic into the onion mixture. Cook for a further 3 minutes before adding the blended tomato along with all the ground spices to the pan, then stir well.

5. Make sure you drain the water from the red kidney beans and then add them to the pan along with the 300ml of fresh water.

6. Simmer the curry on a medium-high heat with a lid on for 13-15 minutes until the gravy has thickened.

7. Check the salt levels and add more as required, up to another teaspoon. Finally, stir in the fenugreek. If you want to add fresh coriander, sprinkle this over just before serving.

Himalayan Chicken Thukpa

Preparation time: 20 minutes + 45 minutes for homemade chicken stock
Cooking time: 25 minutes
Serves 4

For the spice paste

1 small red onion, chopped

5 cloves of garlic, chopped

2.5-5cm (1-2 inches) fresh ginger, peeled and chopped

4 medium tomatoes, chopped

1 fresh green or red chilli (optional)

For the thukpa

2 tbsp vegetable or rapeseed oil

Pinch of asafoetida powder

1 tsp salt

250g chicken, chopped into 1.5-2cm pieces

2 carrots, chopped into 1.5cm pieces

120g fine green beans, chopped into 1.5cm pieces

1.2 litres chicken stock

½ tsp ground turmeric

1 tsp ground cumin

1 tsp ground garam masala

1 tsp Sichuan or black peppercorns, finely crushed

1 lime, juiced

3 heaped tbsp finely chopped fresh coriander, including stalks

4 portions of egg noodles

Chicken thukpa is a Himalayan soup found in the northern states of India including Sikkim, Darjeeling and Ladakh, as well as neighbouring Tibet, Nepal and Bhutan. It's a cross between a chicken noodle soup and a ramen and 'thuk' means heart, so this is a bowl of heart-warming soup. I often make this when I have leftover chicken from a roast dinner which works well, or you can use breast or boned thighs. I also make my homemade chicken stock with the roast chicken carcass (see notes below) but you can use store-bought instead.

1. If you are using homemade chicken stock, begin by following my recipe in the note below.

2. For the spice paste, place all the ingredients into a mini blender and blend until smooth.

3. For the thukpa, heat the oil in a deep pan on a medium heat. When hot, add the asafoetida, which will immediately start sizzling and has a pungent smell that transforms completely once it hits hot oil.

4. Add the spice paste and salt to the pan and cook on a medium-low heat until the raw smell of the paste dissipates completely. This should take around 6 minutes.

5. If you are using raw chicken, add it to the pan now and stir to cover with the paste. Add a drop more oil if needed.

6. After a couple of minutes, add the carrots and green beans, followed by the chicken stock, turmeric, cumin and garam masala. Simmer gently for 5 minutes.

7. Add the peppercorns, lime juice and 2 heaped tablespoons of the fresh coriander. If you're using leftover cooked chicken, add this now as well. Gently simmer for a further 10 minutes.

8. Meanwhile, prepare the egg noodles in a separate pan according to the instructions on the packet. Once the noodles are cooked, drain them and divide into equal portions between serving bowls.

9. Ladle the soup over the noodles, then top with the remaining fresh coriander. Optionally, add extra wedges of lime for squeezing over and, if like me you love Sichuan pepper, an extra dusting of crushed Sichuan pepper before serving.

Notes: To make homemade chicken stock for this recipe, place 1 chicken carcass, half a large leek (roughly chopped), 1 large red chilli (sliced in half), 2 bay leaves, 2 star anise, 1 teaspoon of black peppercorns and 1 whole garlic bulb (halved, no need to peel) in a deep pan and cover with water. Bring to the boil, simmer for 45 minutes, then strain the liquid and discard the solids.

Palak Dal

Preparation time: 10 minutes + 30 minutes soaking
Cooking time: 30 minutes
Serves 4

225g yellow moong/mung lentils

900ml cold water

1 tbsp vegetable or rapeseed oil

1 small dried red chilli OR 1 fresh green chilli, slit lengthways (optional)

1 tsp cumin seeds

¼ tsp asafoetida powder (optional)

½ medium white onion, finely diced

1 heaped tsp finely grated fresh ginger or ginger paste

1 heaped tsp finely grated garlic or garlic paste

2 large tomatoes, finely diced

225g fresh spinach leaves, washed and finely sliced

½ tsp ground turmeric

½ tsp Kashmiri chilli powder

½ lemon, juiced

1 tsp salt, or to taste

Palak dal is a delicious, healthy spinach dal that can be made with a variety of different lentils. While I tend to make mine with yellow moong, also known as yellow mung, you can also make it with toor or red split lentils, known as masoor dal. It is a highly nutritious vegan meal thanks to the combination of lentils and spinach, which also give the dal great contrasting colours of bright green and turmeric yellow.

1. If you have time, first soak the lentils in a bowl of cold water for 30 minutes. This will speed up the cooking time. Drain before cooking.

2. Place the lentils in a deep saucepan and cover with more cold water. Use your hands to massage them for 10 seconds, then pour away the water and repeat to clean them.

3. Cover the lentils with the 900ml of fresh water and leave them to simmer on a medium heat, so the water is gently bubbling, for 15-20 minutes. During cooking, the lentils will expand and soften. If you need to top up the water, add a little at a time. Note that you never drain dal! It is down to personal choice how thick you like your dal so adjust the liquid accordingly.

4. Remove any scum that may form on the surface throughout the cooking process and discard. After 15-20 minutes the lentils should have softened. Check by pressing one between your thumb and forefinger. They should squash easily and not retain any bite. Cook for longer if they remain hard, adding more boiling water if needed.

5. Meanwhile, heat the oil in a deep-sided frying pan or a kadai (India's version of a wok) and then add the dried or fresh chilli if using, followed by the cumin seeds and asafoetida.

6. Allow the cumin seeds to fizzle in the oil for 20 seconds before adding the onion. Cook on a medium-low heat for 4-5 minutes so that it lightly bronzes before adding the ginger and garlic. Cook for another 2 minutes, then add the tomatoes and soften for 3-4 minutes.

7. Add the spinach followed by the ground turmeric and Kashmiri chilli. Add a splash of water to help the spinach wilt if required. Leave to simmer for 3-5 minutes.

8. Blitz the spiced spinach mixture with a handheld blender to make a smooth purée, then stir this into the lentils. If you prefer more texture, you can mix the spinach straight in without blending, but typically I like to blitz it.

9. Add the lemon juice and salt to the dal and taste to check the balance. Salt does bring out the full flavours of the dal so make sure you have added enough before serving.

Dill Dal

Preparation time: 10 minutes + 30 minutes soaking
Cooking time: 25 minutes
Serves 4-6

225g yellow moong/mung dal

2 tbsp vegetable oil

1 tsp brown or black mustard seeds

1 tsp cumin seeds

¼ tsp asafoetida powder

2 dried red chillies

1 tsp finely grated fresh ginger or ginger paste

1 fresh green chilli, finely chopped

½ tsp ground turmeric

1 tsp ground coriander

1 tsp ground cumin

900ml cold water

1 tsp salt, or to taste

30g fresh dill leaves, finely chopped

Occasionally I receive little tasting bowls of whatever is on the stove out the back at one of my favourite grocery stores in Tooting, run by brothers Rohit and Arun. It's always vegetarian and guaranteed to be delicious. I was given a bowl of dill dal the other day and I knew that it had to go into this book. They reeled off what was in it and what I needed to do, so I went home and made it to their exact specifications. It is dal perfection and deliciously unique thanks to the addition of dill instead of coriander.

1. First, soak the dal in a bowl of cold water for 30 minutes. This will speed up the cooking time and aid digestion. Drain them and keep them to hand in the bowl. The next part of the cooking process happens very quickly, so it's important to have everything ready to prevent any of the spices burning which would ruin the whole dish.

2. Put the oil into a medium-size deep pan on a low heat. When hot, add the mustard seeds and cumin seeds. They will begin to splutter and pop so be careful as you add the asafoetida and dried red chillies immediately after.

3. Cook the spices for 10 seconds, then stir in the ginger and green chilli. After 30 seconds, add the ground turmeric, coriander and cumin. They can easily burn so move them around in the oil for 10 seconds, then add the drained lentils and water. Stir well.

4. Leave the dal to simmer on a medium heat for 15-20 minutes, after which time the lentils should be ready. Check by squeezing one between your thumb and forefinger. They should be completely soft. If you find they need a little longer, keep cooking the dal on a low heat and add a little more hot water if it seems to be drying up.

5. Once the lentils have sufficiently softened, add the salt. Salt is integral for bringing flavour to the dal so don't forget it here.

6. Finally, stir the fresh dill into the dal. Simmer gently for a final 5 minutes, adding more water to loosen if required. It is down to personal taste how watery or thick you like your dal.

Punjabi Chole

Preparation time: 5 minutes
Cooking time: 15-20 minutes
Serves 4

2 tbsp vegetable or rapeseed oil

½ tsp cumin seeds

½ tsp fennel seeds

1 star anise

4 cloves

4 green cardamom pods, opened slightly

5cm (2 inch) cinnamon stick, broken in two or three pieces

1 white onion, finely chopped

1 tsp salt

2 tsp ginger-garlic paste (see page 220)

1 fresh green chilli, halved diagonally (optional)

4 medium-size tomatoes, blended until smooth

½ tsp ground turmeric

¼ tsp Kashmiri chilli powder

1 tsp ground coriander

1 tsp chaat masala powder

1 x 400g tin or jar of chickpeas, drained

200ml water

1 tsp sugar

½ tsp ground garam masala

1 tbsp dried fenugreek leaves

2 tbsp chopped fresh coriander leaves

½ small red onion, thinly sliced (optional)

Chickpeas, known as chole or chana, are a great option if you go for the tinned or jarred variety and you want a quick and easy meal. This one literally takes 20 minutes and is cooked in the North Indian style. Typically, it is made with dried chickpeas, which are soaked overnight and then boiled with a few spices and often a teabag or two (to give it that deep brown colour). My version is pared down on time, but not flavour, and is a family favourite.

1. Heat the oil in a wide, deep pan and when hot, add the cumin and fennel seeds. They will immediately begin to sizzle so move them around the pan.

2. After 10 seconds, add the star anise, cloves, green cardamom pods and cinnamon stick, followed swiftly by the white onion and salt. Keep the heat low and allow the onion to lightly bronze, which will take around 6-8 minutes.

3. Now add the ginger-garlic paste and green chilli, if using, and move around the pan for a couple of minutes before adding the blended tomatoes. Leave to simmer for 3 minutes.

4. Add all the ground spices, except the garam masala, which you will add at the end. Stir well and let the mixture simmer gently.

5. Add the chickpeas and water to loosen everything. Place a lid on the pan and leave to simmer for 5 minutes, then stir in the sugar. Taste it to see if you want any more salt. If it remains quite thick, add a little more water to loosen.

6. Finally, add the garam masala and fenugreek, using your thumb and forefinger to break it up and release its aroma as you scatter it into the pan.

7. To serve the chole, top with the fresh coriander and thinly sliced red onion, if using.

Notes: If you are feeding this to more than 4 people, simply add an extra 400g tin or jar of chickpeas. You do not need to increase the quantity of spices, just add a little extra water to loosen the sauce.

Butternut Yellow Mung Dal

**Preparation time: 10 minutes +
30 minutes soaking
Cooking time: 20 minutes
Serves 4**

225g yellow mung lentils

225g butternut squash, peeled and cut into 2.5cm (1 inch) cubes

900ml cold water

1 tbsp vegetable or rapeseed oil

2 small dried red chillies

2 Indian bay leaves

1 tsp panch phoron/Bengali five spice or cumin seeds

1 tsp ground turmeric

¼ tsp Kashmiri chilli powder

1-2 tsp salt

1 tsp ghee

3 cloves of garlic, finely sliced

Handful of fresh coriander, to serve

1 lemon, cut into wedges

Yellow mung dal, also referred to as yellow moong, is versatile and quick to prepare as it does not involve any soaking. Butternut squash, or pumpkin, is perfect in this dal. It uses the Bengali five spice panch phoron, which is a combination of fennel, fenugreek, nigella, black or brown mustard and cumin seeds. See page 218 in the Spice Blends chapter to make your own. This combo is packed full of flavour and goodness, making this dal truly memorable.

1. First, soak the dal in a bowl of cold water for 30 minutes. This will speed up the cooking time and aid digestion.

2. Pour out the water and then cover the drained lentils with the 900ml of fresh cold water and add the cubed butternut squash to the pan.

3. Simmer the lentils and squash gently for 15-20 minutes, removing and discarding the scum that will form on the top. You will likely have to top up the dal with boiling water once or twice as the lentils soak it up. I like my dal to have a soupy consistency, but it's down to personal taste. Once both the dal and butternut have softened, turn off the heat.

4. Now you need to prepare the tempering spices, also known as tadka. Heat the oil in a small frying pan on a low heat and add the chillies and Indian bay leaves.

5. After a minute add the panch phoron or cumin seeds, ground turmeric and Kashmiri chilli powder. It is very important that the panch phoron does not burn, as it will ruin the taste of the whole dal, so keep a close eye on it at this stage.

6. After 20 seconds, mix a couple of tablespoons of the dal into the spices in the pan. Now pour the contents of the spice pan into the dal. Give it a good stir, add the salt and check the taste. If required, add a little sugar to balance it all.

7. Finally – and this part is optional but will give the dal a buttery decadence – heat the small frying pan once more and add the ghee. Stir in the garlic slices and allow them to bronze; this will take no time so keep a close eye on them. As soon as they turn bronze, pour the garlic slices over the dal and serve it with some fresh coriander and a squeeze of lemon.

Notes: Butternut yellow mung dal is pictured on page 31.

Sri Lankan Coconut Dal

Preparation time: 15 minutes (this includes making the curry powder)
Cooking time: 20 minutes
Serves 4-6

2 tbsp coconut or vegetable or rapeseed oil

1 small red onion, roughly chopped

3 cloves of garlic, roughly chopped

7.5cm (3 inch) pandan leaf, halved lengthways

10 curry leaves

1 large tomato, diced

1 heaped tsp Sri Lankan unroasted curry powder (see page 216)

½ tsp ground turmeric

½ tsp freshly ground black pepper

½ tsp chilli powder

1 fresh green chilli, halved lengthways

300g red split lentils

1 x 400ml tin of coconut milk

600ml water

1-2 tsp salt, to taste

This much-loved Sri Lankan dal is so delicious and simple; it literally takes care of itself once you have put all the ingredients in the pan. The only ingredient that may be tricky to source is the pandan leaves, but any Asian grocer will have them, or you can order them online. I buy a few, freeze them and cook with them from frozen. They bring a wonderfully distinct flavour to the dal, but don't worry if you can't find them as it will still taste great.

1. Add the oil to a medium-size deep pan on a medium-low heat and when hot, add the onion. Move the onion around the pan for 3-4 minutes so that it softens and the raw smell dissipates. You do not need it to bronze for this recipe.

2. Add the garlic, pandan leaf, curry leaves, diced tomato, Sri Lankan unroasted curry powder, ground turmeric, black pepper, chilli powder and green chilli. Move them around the pan so that everything is well mixed.

3. Rinse the red split lentils thoroughly under cold water and then add them to the pan along with the coconut milk and water. Mix all the ingredients together.

4. Simmer the dal gently on a medium-low heat for 15-20 minutes, stirring intermittently. The lentils will soften completely and lighten in colour.

5. Once it has cooked, add the salt and a little more water to the dal until it reaches your preferred consistency. There is no correct consistency for dal; it's down to personal choice. I tend to like it more on the loose side than being too thick, but it is totally up to you.

Notes: Sri Lankan coconut dal is pictured on page 35.

Sambar

Preparation time: 15 minutes + 30 minutes soaking
Cooking time: 50 minutes
Serves 4-6

200g toor dal

900ml cold water

45g tamarind pulp (from a block) or 1-2 tsp tamarind concentrate paste

1.1 litres boiling water

2 tbsp vegetable or rapeseed oil

1 large white onion, finely chopped

1 tsp salt

3 okra, chopped into 1-2cm (½ inch) pieces

2 medium tomatoes, finely chopped

1 carrot, finely chopped

½ drumstick/moringa, scrubbed and chopped into 4cm (1.5 inch) pieces (optional, see Fresh Ingredients on page 20)

1 fresh green chilli, sliced down the middle

2 heaped tsp sambar powder/masala (see page 214)

½ tsp ground turmeric

For the tempering

1 tbsp sunflower oil or ghee

2 dried red chillies

1 tsp cumin seeds

1 tsp black mustard seeds

⅛ tsp fenugreek/methi seeds

10-15 curry leaves

Pinch of asafoetida powder

Sambar is an integral part of South Indian and Sri Lankan cuisine, typically served alongside dosa or idli at breakfast but often available from dawn to dusk because it's such a versatile dish. It is deliciously comforting and warming and slightly thinner in consistency than your typical dal. There are so many varieties of sambar and no set rules on which vegetables you need to use. Typically, it includes drumstick (also known as moringa) and carrot, but potato, runner and green beans, turnip, swede and okra work really well too. Use whatever is in season and easy to come by.

1. After soaking the toor dal for 30 minutes, rinse through with cold water and cover with 900ml of fresh water in a saucepan, then bring to the boil. Simmer on a medium heat for 40 minutes or until soft when you squeeze a lentil between your thumb and forefinger. You may need to add more water if it all gets soaked up. Scum will form on top so remove this with a spoon and discard.

2. Once the dal is soft, use a handheld blender or potato masher to lightly blend or mash the lentils until smooth. Set aside off the heat.

3. Meanwhile, put the tamarind pulp in a small bowl and cover with 200ml of the boiling water. Use the back of a spoon to break up the tamarind. Leave to soak for 15 minutes before straining the liquid through a sieve and discarding the stones. Use the back of a spoon to separate the paste from the stones and scrape any extra tamarind paste off the underside of the sieve. Set this paste and liquid mixture aside. If using tamarind concentrate paste, ignore this step.

4. Heat the oil in a deep pan, then add the onion and salt. Allow it to soften for 5 minutes, stirring intermittently, before adding the rest of the vegetables and green chilli. Move around for a couple of minutes and then add the sambar powder and ground turmeric.

5. Add the remaining 900ml of boiling water and the tamarind mixture or paste, then simmer gently for 15 minutes. Once the vegetables have softened, add the lentil mash to the pan and stir well so that it is all combined.

6. For the tempering, put the oil or ghee in a small pan and when hot, add the dried red chillies, cumin, mustard and fenugreek seeds, curry leaves and finally the asafoetida.

7. Move the spices around the pan for 20 seconds and then pour the contents into the pan of sambar. Stir well and taste to check whether you need a little more salt before serving.

Hot and Sour Rasam Soup

Preparation time: 5-10 minutes
Cooking time: 10-15 minutes
Serves 4

45g tamarind pulp (from a block) or
1-2 tsp tamarind concentrate paste

200ml boiling water

1 tbsp vegetable or rapeseed oil

1 tsp brown or black mustard seeds

10 curry leaves

6 button mushrooms, halved (optional)

2 medium-size tomatoes, quartered

2 heaped tsp rasam powder (see
page 214)

1 tsp salt, or to taste

1 litre boiling water

2 tbsp finely chopped fresh coriander,
including stalks

½ fresh lime, juiced

Rasam soup comes from the southern states of India and a steaming bowl of it is both nourishing and heart-warming. The name means 'juice' and as such this soup is meant to be very watery. The rasam powder on page 214 takes minutes to make and then you have a small batch ready for whenever you feel like a pick-me-up. I love a bowl of this zingy hot soup when I need an inner body boost as it really warms you up from the inside, especially when it rains. For me, a lunchtime version with added mushrooms offers great comfort.

1. If you are using tamarind pulp from a block, tear off 45g (a small golf ball size) and place in a bowl. Cover with the 200ml of boiling water and use the back of a spoon to break it up a little. Leave for 10 minutes. If you're using tamarind paste, it doesn't need soaking.

2. Heat the oil in a medium-size saucepan and when hot, add the mustard seeds, followed by the curry leaves. Allow them to sizzle in the pan for 20 seconds and then add the mushrooms, if using, and move them around the pan for a couple of minutes.

3. Add the quartered tomatoes, rasam powder and salt. Pour the soaked tamarind pulp through a sieve into the pan, using the back of a spoon to push through any remaining tamarind pulp and a spatula to scrape off any on the underside of the sieve. Alternatively, stir in the first teaspoon of tamarind concentrate paste.

4. Add the litre of boiling water to the pan, give everything a stir and simmer the soup gently for 10 minutes.

5. Finally, add the fresh coriander and lime juice and then do a taste test to check the sourness and salt levels. Add a little more rasam powder, salt or tamarind concentrate paste if required before serving. The salty, sour and hot flavours should be nicely balanced.

VEGETABLES

Being vegetarian would be a breeze in India. There are myriad possibilities when it comes to vegetable dishes. Spices transform even the humblest of vegetables. As more of the world is becoming more vegetarian in their eating habits, I thought it was important to have a large section showcasing some of the vegetarian Indian dishes my family eat regularly. I have largely focused on vegetables that are commonplace in the West and hence readily available here in the UK. Such stalwarts as cabbages, beans and cauliflower really benefit from Indian culinary techniques, most of which are disarmingly simple.

Courgette and Tomato Curry

Preparation time: 15 minutes
Cooking time: 35 minutes
Serves 4

2 tbsp vegetable or rapeseed oil

1 tsp cumin seeds

1 tsp fennel seeds

2 small dried red chillies

1 medium-size red onion, roughly chopped

1 tsp salt

1 heaped tsp finely grated or chopped garlic, or garlic paste

1 heaped tsp finely grated or chopped fresh ginger, or ginger paste

3 large ripe tomatoes, finely chopped

1 tsp ground turmeric

1 tsp ground coriander

1 tsp ground cumin

½ tsp Kashmiri chilli powder (less if you are using a different chilli powder)

100-200ml water (if your tomatoes are juicy, you may require less)

2 large courgettes, halved lengthways and then cut into 1.5cm half moons

½ tsp ground garam masala

2 tbsp fresh coriander, roughly chopped

I always have a glut of courgettes in my fridge, so this is a great way of using them up. It's quick to prepare and uses a combination of whole and dried spices. The quantity of water in this recipe depends on the ripeness of your tomatoes to make the gravy. The courgettes themselves take minutes to soften and then it's finished with a sprinkling of garam masala and some fresh coriander. I love to eat a bowl of this on its own, but it also works well as part of a larger Indian feast.

1. Using a wide pan with a lid, heat the oil on a medium-low heat and when hot, add the cumin and fennel seeds and the dried chillies. Move them around the pan for 15 seconds, being careful not to let them burn, then add the onion and salt.

2. Stir the whole spices and onions together, then gently fry for around 5-6 minutes so that the onion softens and begins to bronze.

3. Stir the garlic and ginger into the onion and spices, cook for another couple of minutes, stirring intermittently, then add the chopped tomatoes followed by the ground turmeric, coriander, cumin and Kashmiri chilli powder.

4. Place a lid on the pan and leave everything to soften for 5 minutes. During this time, give the tomatoes a stir intermittently and add 100ml of the water to loosen as required. You are aiming for an unctuous tomato gravy as opposed to a dry curry. It will seem quite watery at first but will reduce a great deal before you finish cooking.

5. Now add the courgettes and fold them into the tomato gravy along with the final 100ml of water if needed, depending on how juicy the tomatoes are.

6. Keep the pan on a medium heat so that the courgettes soften completely and the gravy reduces and thickens. Place a lid on the pan and simmer for 10-15 minutes.

7. Finally, taste test for the salt levels and then when you are satisfied with the flavour, fold in the garam masala and fresh chopped coriander just before serving.

Aubergine and Tamarind Curry

Preparation time: 15 minutes
Cooking time: 40 minutes
Serves 4

4 cloves

5 black peppercorns

8 green cardamon pods

1 tsp cumin seeds

1 tsp coriander seeds

8 tbsp vegetable or rapeseed oil

2 aubergines, cut into 2cm cubes

1 tsp black or brown mustard seeds

15 curry leaves

1 medium-size white onion, finely chopped

1 tsp finely grated garlic or garlic paste

1 tsp finely grated fresh ginger or ginger paste

45g tamarind pulp (from a block) or 1-2 tsp tamarind concentrate paste

300g fresh tomatoes

1 tsp Kashmiri chilli powder

1 x 400ml tin of coconut milk

1 tsp salt, or to taste

1 tsp sugar, or to taste

This unctuous South Indian curry is sweet, sour, tangy and smoky: a delicious way to cook aubergine. You will find blocks of tamarind pulp in large supermarkets and Asian grocers, and it stores easily in the fridge for months. If you can't find it, you can use tamarind paste but will only need 1-2 teaspoons as it is far more concentrated. There are a few stages to making this curry, but the result is well worth it.

1. Dry roast the whole spices (cloves, peppercorns, cardamom pods, cumin and coriander seeds) in a large frying pan for a minute and then blend them, including the cardamom husks, or use a pestle and mortar to form a powder.

2. Next, add 3 tablespoons of the oil to your pan and fry half of the cubed aubergine so that it softens and browns, then repeat this with 3 more tablespoons of oil and the remaining aubergine. It will take around 6 minutes per batch and you may find you need to add more oil during the frying process. Remove the fried aubergine with a slotted spoon and set aside.

3. Heat a wok or other wide pan which is deeper than the frying pan. Add the remaining 2 tablespoons of oil and when hot, add the mustard seeds and curry leaves. The mustard seeds will begin to pop immediately so be careful. Add the onion and keep the heat on medium-low to let the onion soften and bronze, which will take around 6-8 minutes.

4. Add the garlic and ginger to the pan and cook for another few minutes, then add the freshly ground spice mix and stir into the onions.

5. Meanwhile, place the tamarind pulp in a small bowl and cover it with boiling water. Break up with the back of a spoon and leave to soak for 10 minutes. If you are using tamarind paste, skip this step.

6. Blend the fresh tomatoes to form a smooth paste and then add them to the onion mixture in the pan. Simmer for 5 minutes and then add the Kashmiri chilli powder.

7. Pour the soaked tamarind pulp into a sieve over a bowl and use a spoon to push the pulp through as much as possible. Scrape the paste into the bowl from the bottom of the sieve and discard any solids left in the top. Pour the contents of the bowl into the pan. If you are using tamarind paste, simply add this to the pan now.

8. Add the fried aubergines and coconut milk to the pan and then gently simmer for 10 minutes. You may need to add a little more water to loosen the sauce if necessary.

9. Finally, add the salt and sugar to balance out the curry. Taste to check whether you need to add more, then simmer for a few minutes before serving.

Keralan Cauliflower and Coconut Milk Curry

Preparation time: 15 minutes
Cooking time: 30 minutes
Serves 4-6

1 medium or large cauliflower

4 tbsp coconut or rapeseed oil

1 heaped tsp cumin seeds

1 heaped tsp black or brown mustard seeds

1-2 dried red chillies

1 white onion, finely chopped

1 tsp salt

1 heaped tsp finely grated garlic or garlic paste

1 heated tsp finely grated fresh ginger or ginger paste

1 tsp ground cumin

1 tsp ground coriander

1 tsp ground turmeric

1 tsp Kashmiri chilli powder

3 large tomatoes, finely chopped

1 x 400ml tin of full-fat coconut milk

100ml water

1 tsp brown sugar or jaggery (optional)

Fresh coriander, to serve (optional)

Toasted coconut shavings, to serve (optional)

Cauliflower has been a staple in Indian cuisine forever. Here in the West, it is enjoying a recent elevation to 'superfood' status. I always use the outer leaves too: just wash them thoroughly and then chop them finely. This recipe is from the South Indian state of Kerala and although it includes both dried chillies and chilli powder, it is cooled by the sweet notes of the coconut milk. I remember having very similar curries during my visit to the Keralan backwaters.

1. First, prepare the cauliflower by finely chopping the outer leaves (if it has any) and halving or quartering the florets so the pieces are evenly sized.

2. Heat half of the oil in a wide pan of medium depth, then add the cauliflower florets (not the green leaves yet) in batches so that they begin to lightly bronze. This will take around 4-5 minutes per batch. Transfer the cauliflower to a bowl and set aside.

3. Using the same pan and the remaining oil, heat the cumin and mustard seeds and the dried chillies. After 20 seconds, add the onion and salt. Allow the onion to soften and begin to bronze for around 6-8 minutes.

4. Add the garlic and ginger, stirring them into the spices and onion, then add the ground cumin, coriander, turmeric and Kashmiri chilli powder, followed by the chopped tomatoes.

5. Allow the tomatoes to break down for the next 3 minutes, then return the cauliflower florets to the pan along with the finely chopped leaves.

6. Pour the coconut milk and water into the pan, stir all the ingredients together and then leave the curry to simmer on a medium heat, covered, for 7-10 minutes or until the cauliflower has softened sufficiently. Test this with a sharp knife.

7. Taste test the sauce, adding the sugar or jaggery if you like along with more salt if necessary. Let it simmer for another minute.

8. To serve, scatter the curry with a handful of fresh coriander and/or toasted coconut shavings according to your preference.

Nigella Seed, Sprout and Carrot Curry

Preparation time: 15 minutes
Cooking time: 15 minutes
Serves 4

2 tbsp vegetable or rapeseed oil

1 tsp nigella seeds

1 fresh green chilli, finely sliced widthways

325g sprouts, finely sliced

300g carrots, grated

1 tsp ground turmeric

1 tsp salt

50ml water

Love them or loathe them, this curry may win over even the most diehard of sprout haters. It's a Bengali recipe and I distinctly remember the first time I ate it. The sprouts looked nothing like sprouts as they had been finely sliced, and marrying them with the sweet carrot and spices really transforms them into a memorable dish. There are very few ingredients, so it is easy to whip together. You can serve this simply with a dollop of yoghurt and some fresh coriander to make a super tasty lunch or supper.

1. Heat the oil in a medium-size deep pan and when hot, add the nigella seeds. They will immediately begin to sizzle in the pan.

2. After 15 seconds, add the fresh chilli and give it a little stir. After a further 10 seconds, add the finely sliced sprouts and grated carrots.

3. Stir to coat the vegetables with the nigella seeds and green chilli. Add the ground turmeric and salt and continue to stir on a medium heat so that the carrots and sprouts soften but do not burn. Use a wooden spoon to press down on the ingredients as you gently stir.

4. After 3 minutes, add the water and stir into the curry. Allow the sprouts and carrots to soften. Stir intermittently, adding a little more water if it becomes too dry, for the next 5-7 minutes. If you place a lid on the pan the moisture from the steam will help cook the sprouts and carrots quicker.

5. Within 10 minutes it will be ready to eat. Check the salt levels and add more if required.

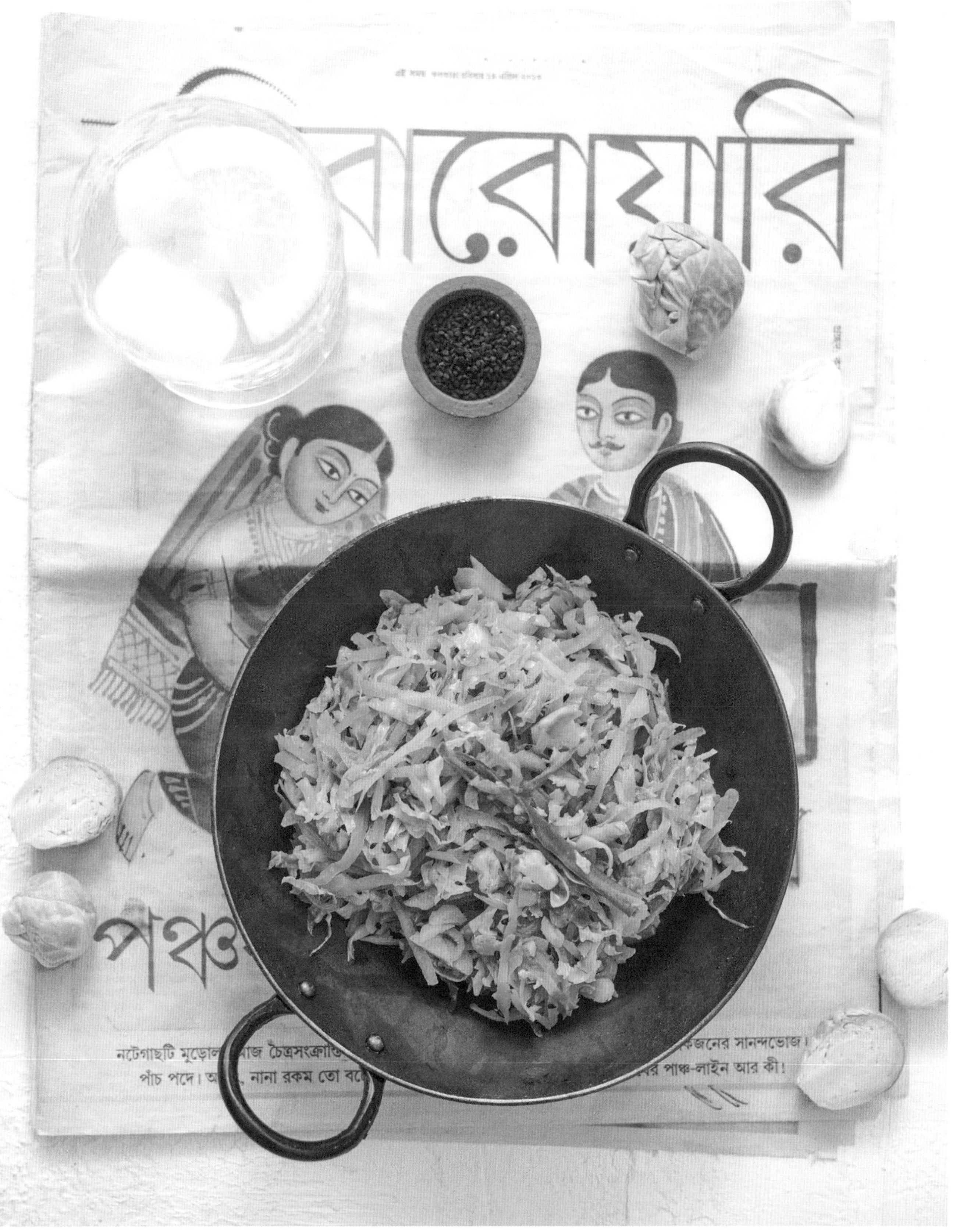

Beetroot Curry

Preparation time: 15 minutes
Cooking time: 30 minutes
Serves 4

1 tbsp coconut or rapeseed oil

½ red onion, roughly chopped

½ tsp salt

2 cloves of garlic, thinly sliced lengthways

10 curry leaves

1 x 7.5cm (3 inch) pandan leaf, halved lengthways

1 medium tomato, roughly chopped

1 tsp ground garam masala

¼ tsp ground turmeric

¼ tsp Kashmiri chilli powder

Pinch of freshly ground black pepper

3 medium or large beetroot, peeled and cut into thin 5cm (2 inch) batons

25ml water

200ml full-fat coconut milk

This curry completely transforms beetroot and has been known to convince those who would normally overlook this nutritious vegetable. Its origin stems from southern India and Sri Lanka, where I was taught to cook it by some locals. The pandan leaf has a unique flavour that really adds to this curry so is worth sourcing. You can find them in Asian grocers or online. Like curry leaves, you can store them in the freezer and cook directly from frozen.

1. Begin by gently warming the oil in a medium-size pan. Add the red onion, salt, sliced garlic, curry leaves, pandan leaf and fresh tomato. The wonderous smells from the pan will come from the pandan and curry leaves, which really make this curry something memorable.

2. Move everything around the pan and allow them to gently soften for 5 minutes. You do not need to bronze the onion, simply soften it.

3. Next, stir in the ground spices: garam masala, turmeric, Kashmiri chilli powder and black pepper. After 2-3 minutes, add the beetroot batons and stir them into the mixture.

4. Pour in the water and coconut milk and stir once again so all the ingredients are coating the beetroot. Simmer gently for around 20 minutes to soften the beetroot and reduce the liquid. Stir intermittently and add a little more water if required to cook the beetroot.

5. Taste the curry to check the beetroot has softened sufficiently and add more salt and/or fresh ground pepper as required before serving.

Bengali Egg Curry

Preparation time: 10 minutes
Cooking time: 20 minutes
Serves 4

5 hard-boiled eggs

¼ tsp ground turmeric

½ tsp Kashmiri chilli powder

3 tbsp vegetable or rapeseed or mustard oil

1 tsp cumin seeds

2 Indian bay leaves

1 medium white onion, finely chopped or blended

1 tsp salt

2 fresh green chillies, finely chopped or 2 dried red chillies, kept whole

2 tsp ginger-garlic paste (see page 220)

4 tomatoes, finely chopped or 200ml tinned tomatoes

½ tsp sugar, or to taste

½ tsp Kashmiri chilli powder

½ tsp ground turmeric

1 tsp ground coriander

250ml water

1 tsp ground garam masala

When I visit relatives in Kolkata I'm often woken up by the egg and milk seller as he pushes his cart along the street outside. I rather like the way he calls up 'dim' (meaning egg) in a long harmonious "diiiiiiimmmmm" sound followed by 'dut' (meaning milk), again a rather elongated "duuuuuuuuuut". I became a huge fan of egg curry the first time I ate it and have cooked it regularly ever since. Typically, Bengalis would cook this dish with mustard oil, but if you find it hard to source, then use vegetable or rapeseed oil, which works just fine.

1. Once you have hard-boiled the eggs, remove the shells and then lightly make two incisions on either side of each egg. This will allow the spices and aromatics to work their way into the eggs during the cooking process.

2. Place the prepared eggs in a bowl and sprinkle over the ground turmeric and Kashmiri chilli powder to completely coat them.

3. Using a deep pan or wok, heat 1 tablespoon of the oil and then add the spiced eggs. Move them continually around the pan for 2 minutes so that they lightly bronze. Remove from the oil with a slotted spoon and place to one side.

4. Heat the remaining oil in the same pan and then add the cumin seeds and Indian bay leaves. Move them around the pan for 20 seconds and then add the onion, salt and chillies.

5. Allow the onion to lightly bronze on a low heat for 6-8 minutes and then add the ginger-garlic paste. Stir this into the onion for 2 minutes.

6. Add the tomatoes, sugar, Kashmiri chilli powder, ground turmeric and coriander to the pan. Stir for 30 seconds before adding the water, then place a lid on the pan and simmer on a low heat for 5 minutes.

7. Return the eggs to the pan and coat them in the gravy. Cover with a lid once again and simmer for a further 3 minutes. Add more water as required if the sauce looks dry.

8. Sprinkle over the garam masala and fold it gently into the curry before serving.

Unripe Jackfruit Curry

Preparation time: 10 minutes
Cooking time: 30-35 minutes
Serves 4-6

2 tins of young green jackfruit (500g combined weight once drained)

2 tbsp vegetable or rapeseed oil

1 tsp cumin seeds

½ tsp brown or black mustard seeds

¼ tsp asafoetida powder

2 Indian bay leaves/tej patta

1-2 small dried red chillies (optional)

1 small red or white onion, finely chopped

1 tsp salt, or to taste

1 tsp finely grated garlic or garlic paste

1 tsp finely grated fresh ginger or ginger paste

1 tsp ground coriander

1 tsp ground turmeric

½ tsp ground cumin

½ tsp Kashmiri chilli powder (less if you are using a regular chilli powder)

4 large fresh tomatoes, blended

300ml water

½ tsp sugar

½ tsp ground garam masala

Handful of fresh coriander, roughly chopped including stalks

The first time I tasted unripe, young, raw jackfruit (known as echor in Bengali) was in a curry at a family celebration in Kolkata. My husband's "mama" (maternal uncle) had organised fantastic caterers to prepare a banquet for all the relatives who would be dropping by throughout the day. The curry was exquisitely light and yet had the texture of pulled pork. Jackfruit is fast becoming mainstream in the western diet and while it is possible to source fresh jackfruit in the larger cities, tinned works well for this curry and saves you a lot of time.

1. The unripe jackfruit will come in water or brine so remove it from the tins and drain well (run it under cold water for a minute first if it was in brine).

2. Break up each chunk of jackfruit into 3 or 4 pieces on a chopping board. It will resemble pulled pork or tinned tuna. Leave to one side while you begin the sauce.

3. Using a medium-size deep pan, heat the oil on a medium heat. Add the cumin and mustard seeds followed by the asafoetida powder, Indian bay leaves and dried chillies if using.

4. Move the spices around the pan for 20 seconds and then add the onion and salt. Gently fry for 5 minutes and then add the garlic and ginger. Cook for a further 2 minutes.

5. Now add the ground spices: coriander, turmeric, cumin and Kashmiri chilli powder. Mix them into the onion, garlic and ginger and then add the blended tomatoes.

6. Place a lid on the pan and simmer for 5 minutes. If the sauce becomes very dry, simply add a splash of water to loosen it.

7. Stir the jackfruit into the spiced tomato gravy and simmer for a couple more minutes before adding the water.

8. Simmer on a medium-low heat for 15 minutes, stirring intermittently. The gravy will reduce dramatically: again, add a splash more water if it dries up completely.

9. Add the sugar, garam masala and fresh coriander. Stir them into the curry and then taste test to check whether it requires more salt before serving.

Notes: Do not use sweet yellow jackfruit for this curry, as that is used exclusively for sweet dishes.

Bengali Green Bean and Potato Curry

Preparation time: 15 minutes
Cooking time: 20-25 minutes
Serves 4

2 tbsp vegetable or rapeseed oil

1-2 fresh green chillies, finely chopped

1 tsp nigella seeds

1 red onion, finely diced

1 tsp salt

3 cloves of garlic, roughly chopped

1 large or 2 medium potatoes, peeled and diced into bite-size cubes

350g fine green beans, halved

1 tsp ground turmeric

1 tsp ground coriander

½ tsp Kashmiri chilli powder

1 large or 2 medium tomatoes, diced or 2 tbsp chopped tinned tomatoes

150ml boiling water

½ tsp ground garam masala

This Bengali curry has always been a go-to for my family as fine green beans are a vegetable we always seem to have in the fridge. You can make this with runner beans too, although I would cut them on the diagonal into 2.5cm (1 inch) pieces. Unlike some European recipes where beans retain their crunch, this recipe requires them to be very soft.

1. Heat the oil on a medium heat and when hot, add the fresh green chillies and nigella seeds. Move them around the pan for 15 seconds before adding the onion and salt.

2. Cook the onion on a medium heat, allowing it to soften and lightly bronze over the next 6-8 minutes. Add the garlic and mix well for a couple of minutes.

3. Stir in the diced potatoes, then place a lid on the pan and leave to simmer for 5 minutes.

4. Now add the fine green beans and the ground turmeric, coriander and Kashmiri chilli. Stir them in well before adding the tomatoes and boiling water.

5. Put the lid back on the pan and leave the curry to simmer on a low-medium heat for 10-12 minutes.

6. After this time, check to see if the potato has softened by gently cutting into one cube with a sharp knife. If it is still firm, continue cooking for a little longer. Add a little more water if the sauce is drying up.

7. Once the beans have wilted and are completely soft like the potato, stir the garam masala into the curry. Check the salt levels before serving.

Spicy Potato Curry

Preparation time: 15 minutes
Cooking time: 30 minutes
Serves 4

4 medium potatoes

2 large tomatoes

2.5cm fresh ginger

2 tbsp vegetable or rapeseed oil

1 tsp black or brown mustard seeds

1 tsp cumin seeds

¼ tsp fenugreek seeds

¼ tsp asafoetida powder

2 fresh green chillies, halved

1 tsp salt, or to taste

1 tsp Kashmiri chilli powder

1 tsp amchoor/mango powder

½ tsp ground turmeric

½ tsp ground cumin

400ml water

1 tsp dried fenugreek leaves or
chopped fresh coriander leaves

1 tsp ghee (optional)

Sometimes I crave a warming spiced potato and tomato curry, and this one definitely hits the spot. It does not require onion or garlic and yet is packed full of flavours from the range of spices. It is great eaten on its own but also works well as part of a large spread. Any of the flatbreads in this book (see pages 178 to 182) or basmati rice would work well alongside it.

1. First, peel the potatoes and cut them into 2.5cm (1 inch) cubes. Parboil these until softened but still holding their shape. Drain and then gently crush, but do not mash, the potato.

2. Next, blitz the tomatoes and ginger in a blender until smooth. If you do not have a blender, use 200ml passata or tinned tomatoes with 1 teaspoon of ginger paste.

3. Heat the oil in a deep pan, kadai or wok and when hot, add the mustard, cumin and fenugreek seeds as well as the asafoetida. They will immediately begin to sizzle in the pan so be careful in case they spit.

4. Move the spices around the pan and then add the green chillies. After 20 seconds, add the tomato and ginger purée to the pan and simmer for 3-5 minutes.

5. Add the lightly crushed potatoes to the pan and stir them into the tomato sauce. Add the salt, Kashmiri chilli and mango powders, ground turmeric and cumin. Stir in well.

6. Pour in the water and then simmer gently with the lid on for 10 minutes. After this time, do a taste test and then add the dried fenugreek leaves or fresh coriander.

7. For added decadence, you can stir in a teaspoon of ghee just before serving the curry.

Cauliflower with Potato and Dried Fenugreek

Preparation time: 10 minutes
Cooking time: 30 minutes
Serves 4-6

1 medium-size cauliflower

5 tbsp mustard or vegetable or rapeseed oil

1 tsp ground turmeric

1 tsp cumin seeds

2 Indian bay leaves

3 green cardamom pods, opened slightly

3 cloves

2 small dried red chillies

2 medium potatoes, cut into 1.5-2cm cubes

1 tsp salt, or to taste

1 tsp ground cumin

1 tsp ground coriander

½ tsp Kashmiri chilli powder (optional, less if using a different chilli powder)

140ml water

2 tbsp dried fenugreek leaves/kasoori methi

This cauliflower curry is known as 'phulkopi aloo kasoori methi' in Bengali, literally translating as cauliflower, potato, dried fenugreek leaves. Scattering the dried leaves over the cauliflower at the very end of the cooking and gently folding them in gives the dish a wonderful aroma. I cook this dish with ground turmeric, cumin and coriander too, but my mother-in-law keeps it simpler by just adding oil, dried chillies, salt and kasoori methi. It is also delicious this way, so try both and see which you prefer. Traditionally, mustard oil is used in this recipe, but the alternatives will work fine.

1. First, prepare the cauliflower by finely chopping the outer leaves (if it has any) and halving or quartering the florets so the pieces are evenly sized.

2. Using a large wide pan with a lid, add 3 tablespoons of the oil and when hot, add the cauliflower florets (but not the green leaves) along with half of the ground turmeric.

3. Gently fry for around 6 minutes so that the cauliflower begins to bronze, adding a little more oil if required. Transfer the florets to a bowl and set aside.

4. Using the same pan, heat the remaining oil and then add the cumin seeds, Indian bay leaves, green cardamom, cloves and dried red chillies.

5. Move everything around in the oil for 20 seconds and then add the cubed potato. Fry gently in the pan for 5-6 minutes so it begins to bronze.

6. Add the salt, cumin, coriander, Kashmiri chilli powder and remaining ground turmeric to the pan and then return the cauliflower florets. Fold the spices into the cauliflower and potato.

7. Add the finely chopped outer leaves of the cauliflower and stir well, then pour the water into the pan. Cover with a lid for 10-15 minutes, or until the potato and cauliflower are soft.

8. At the very end of the cooking time, add the dried fenugreek leaves, using your fingers to break up the leaves. Stir in gently, then taste test and add more salt as required.

Courgette, Potato and Pea Sabzi

Preparation time: 15 minutes
Cooking time: 20 minutes
Serves 4

2 medium-size potatoes (360g)

2 large courgettes (560g)

2 tbsp vegetable or rapeseed oil

1 tsp black or brown mustard seeds

¼ tsp asafoetida powder (optional)

1-2 dried red chillies, broken in half

10-15 curry leaves

1 small red onion, diced

1 tsp salt, or to taste

1 large clove of garlic, finely chopped

½ tsp ground turmeric

70g frozen peas

30ml water

Fresh coriander leaves, to garnish

Sabzis are great with any vegetable that needs using up. While this one includes black mustard seeds, you can try using nigella or cumin seeds instead, which will give the dish a completely different flavour. Play around and see which you like best. Equally, you can add fresh instead of dried chillies. It works well as a vegetarian meal on its own, or as part of a larger spread with dal and a meat or fish curry.

1. First, peel the potatoes and cut them into 2.5cm (1 inch) cubes. Parboil these for around 4-5 minutes so that they are still holding their shape, then drain. You do not want to make the potato too soft or it will turn mushy later. Cut the courgettes into cubes of the same size and set both vegetables aside for now.

2. Heat the oil in a medium-size, wide, deep pan with a lid on a low heat. When hot, add the mustard seeds, asafoetida if using, dried red chillies and curry leaves.

3. Add the onion and salt and move everything around the pan for a couple of minutes, then add the garlic. You want the onions to be softened, but not bronzed.

4. Next, add the boiled potatoes and a minute later the courgette, followed by the ground turmeric. Stir gently so that the spices coat the vegetables.

5. After 5 minutes, add the frozen peas and up to 30ml of water, then place a lid on the pan. Stir intermittently and check that the potato has softened sufficiently. It takes around 10-12 minutes if you have it cooking on quite a high heat.

6. Taste the sabzi to check the salt level, then scatter with fresh coriander leaves and serve.

Fine Green Bean Thoran

Preparation time: 15 minutes
Cooking time: 25 minutes
Serves 4

500g fine green beans

1 tbsp coconut or rapeseed oil

½ tsp cumin seeds

½ tsp black or brown mustard seeds

½ tsp urid dal (optional)

10-15 curry leaves

1-2 dried red chillies, broken in two

½ small red onion, finely chopped

1 tsp salt, or to taste

2 tbsp water

½ tsp ground turmeric

½ Kashmiri chilli powder (less if using a different chilli powder)

3 tbsp freshly grated or desiccated coconut

2 cloves of garlic, peeled

1 fresh green chilli

A thoran is a dry vegetable curry, commonly found in the state of Kerala. There is a very similar dish in Tamil Nadu, known as poriyal. Both dishes combine vegetables with coconut. Fresh is best, but desiccated also works well, for convenience. It is a straightforward dish and easy to prepare when you are in a hurry. It also works well alongside more gravy-led curries, creating a balanced meal.

1. Finely chop the green beans and wash them thoroughly in a colander. This will speed up the cooking of the beans later.

2. Heat the oil in a pan on a low heat and when hot, add the cumin and mustard seeds along with the urid dal if using.

3. Allow them to fizzle and pop for a few seconds, then add the curry leaves and dried red chilli. Stir in the onion and salt and allow the onion to soften and become translucent, but not bronzed, over the next 3-4 minutes.

4. Now add the green beans and water followed by the turmeric and Kashmiri chilli. Stir well, keeping the pan on a low heat, then cover with a lid and leave for 10-15 minutes. Stir the mixture a couple of times and then test to see if the beans have softened sufficiently.

5. Meanwhile, make a coarse paste with the grated coconut, peeled garlic cloves and fresh green chilli. You can do this in a chopper or using a pestle and mortar. If you have neither, bashing them with the end of a rolling pin in a metal or plastic bowl will work, although this method will create more of a breadcrumb-like consistency than a paste, which is still fine.

6. Once the beans have softened but retain some bite, add the coarse coconut paste to the pan and stir it in. Simmer for a couple of minutes so that the raw taste of the coconut dissipates.

7. Taste to check the flavour and add more salt if required before serving.

Keralan Cabbage Thoran

Preparation time: 15 minutes
Cooking time: 12-15 minutes
Serves 4

2 tbsp coconut or rapeseed oil

1 tsp brown or black mustard seeds

1-2 small dried red chillies

10-15 curry leaves

1 small red onion, finely diced

2 fresh green chillies, sliced lengthways

1 tsp salt, or to taste

1 tsp ground turmeric

1 tsp grated fresh ginger or ginger paste

½ large white cabbage, finely shredded
(either by hand or using the fine slicer
mode on a Magimix)

20g freshly grated coconut or
desiccated coconut

This dry Keralan cabbage and coconut dish is very different from my Bengali white cabbage recipe. Equally quick and easy, it elevates the humble cabbage into something delicious in no time at all. It proved hugely popular in my online classes as it does really transform a white cabbage into deliciously memorable dish. A good addition to this dish is finely grated carrot.

1. Warm the oil in a karahi, wok or frying pan. The key is to have a really wide, deep pan with a lid as half a cabbage produces more volume than you would think once you have sliced it up.

2. When the oil is hot, add the mustard seeds, dried red chillies and curry leaves. The mustard seeds will begin to pop immediately so be careful.

3. Add the diced red onion, fresh green chillies, salt and ground turmeric. Move everything around the pan, allowing the onion to soften. It does not need to bronze but allow it to soften for 3-4 minutes.

4. Add the ginger to the pan and stir into the other ingredients. After a couple of minutes, add the cabbage to the pan and mix in well. Do not add any water or cover with a lid, as you are stir-frying rather than steaming.

5. After a couple of minutes, add the grated coconut and mix in well. Keep the pan on a medium heat and stir the contents every minute or so. If you find that anything is charring on the bottom, you can add a small splash of water, but try to avoid this if you can.

6. Taste to test whether the cabbage is soft enough and add more salt as required. It should be cooked within 8-10 minutes, providing the cabbage has been finely sliced enough. Continue cooking for a few more minutes if necessary. It should still retain a little bite but should have softened considerably from its raw state.

Okra Sabzi

Preparation time: 15-20 minutes
Cooking time: 20 minutes
Serves 4

Okra, also known as ladies' fingers, is more widely available in the supermarkets than ever and it makes a lovely alternative vegetable to include in your diet. Try and purchase the young and tender pods, which are smaller in size, as they will not be so stringy. This dish is highly nutritious, colourful and really tasty. It is meant to be more of a dry than a saucy curry.

400g okra (young and tender pods are best)

2 tbsp vegetable or rapeseed oil

1 tsp black or brown mustard seeds

10-15 curry leaves

1 fresh green chilli, finely chopped (optional)

1 red onion, finely chopped

1 tsp ground coriander

1 tsp ground cumin

½ tsp ground turmeric

½ tsp ground garam masala

½ tsp Kashmiri chilli powder

5 cloves of garlic, thinly sliced

2 tomatoes, finely chopped

1 tsp salt, or to taste

½ lemon (optional)

1. Wash and dry the okra thoroughly. If you can, do this an hour before you start cooking so they are completely dry. This is an important step as it prevents any sliminess when cooking.

2. Slice the ends off the okra and discard, then cut them widthways into 2cm pieces, or you can slice on the diagonal about three times per pod.

3. Heat the oil in a deep-frying pan or wok on a medium-low heat and when hot, add the mustard seeds, curry leaves, and green chilli if using. The mustard seeds will pop and spit so be careful when you add them to the oil.

4. After 20 seconds, add the onion and keep the pan on a medium heat, moving the onion around the pan gently for about 5 minutes so that it begins to soften.

5. Stir in the ground coriander, cumin, turmeric, garam masala and Kashmiri chilli powder and then add the garlic slices. Cook gently for a further couple of minutes.

6. Add the okra, tomatoes and salt and fold them into all the spices. Do not add a lid as it will create moisture and in turn make the okra slimy. Simmer for 10-15 minutes, moving the okra around the pan until it softens and is ready to eat.

7. Taste test to check the salt levels and adjust accordingly. If you do feel the okra is looking slimy, adding a squeeze of lemon juice will help.

Potato, Pea and Paneer

Preparation time: 15 minutes
Cooking time: 35 minutes
Serves 4, or 6 with other dishes

2 tbsp vegetable or rapeseed oil

500g paneer, cubed

350g fresh tomatoes

1-2 fresh green chillies

1 tbsp each ghee and oil

1 heaped tsp cumin seeds

¼ tsp asafoetida powder

3 Indian bay leaves

1 heaped tsp finely grated fresh ginger or ginger paste

1 tsp finely grated garlic or garlic paste

1 tsp Kashmiri chilli powder

1 tsp ground turmeric

2 tsp ground coriander

200g potatoes, peeled and cut into 2cm cubes

100g frozen peas

500ml water

1 tsp salt, or to taste

1 tsp ground garam masala

Handful of fresh coriander leaves, to serve

This rich, unctuous, tomato-based North Indian vegetarian curry is hugely popular, both in India and in my house. It is often called paneer matar, as matar means pea. Paneer is a mild, unsalted soft cheese that easily absorbs surrounding flavours. While paneer is straightforward to make, I often rely on store-bought packs and today you can find it at most large supermarkets as well as Asian grocers. This is a great vegetarian curry that is packed full of flavour and goodness.

1. Heat the oil in a frying pan and then gently fry the paneer cubes until they are bronzed on one or two sides. This will only take around 5 minutes. Remove with a slotted spoon and place in a bowl. Meanwhile, blitz the tomatoes and green chillies in a chopper until smooth.

2. Heat the ghee and oil in a deep saucepan on a medium heat and when hot, add the cumin seeds, asafoetida and bay leaves. The cumin seeds will immediately begin to sizzle so be careful. Move them around the pan for 20 seconds and then add the ginger and garlic.

3. After 30 seconds add the blended tomato chilli sauce and simmer gently for 5 minutes. Next, stir the Kashmiri chilli powder, ground turmeric and coriander into the gravy.

4. Add the cubed potatoes, paneer and peas to the pan along with the water. Bring to the boil and then simmer gently for 20 minutes or until the potato is soft, stirring intermittently.

5. Add the salt and garam masala, then simmer for a couple more minutes. Scatter with fresh coriander leaves to serve.

Spiced Smoky Aubergine

Preparation time: 10 minutes
Cooking time: 25-60 minutes
Serves 4

2 large aubergines

2 tbsp vegetable or rapeseed oil

1 tsp cumin seeds

1-2 fresh green chillies, finely chopped

1 small red onion, finely chopped

1 heaped tsp finely grated fresh ginger or ginger paste

4 cloves of garlic, finely sliced or chopped

½ tsp Kashmiri chilli powder

½ tsp ground turmeric

½ tsp ground coriander

½ -1 tsp salt, to taste

4 medium-size tomatoes, diced

2 tbsp chopped fresh coriander, to serve

This North Indian aubergine dish, known as baingan bharta, is India's answer to the Middle Eastern baba ganoush. I first ate it in Rajasthan and immediately knew that it was something I wanted to cook back at home. It's comforting and warming and works well on its own, with paratha or chapati, and as part of a larger spread. The aubergines are best cooked over a gas flame or barbecue to give them a smoky aroma. You can soften them in an oven, they just won't have the same smoky edge.

1. Place the whole aubergines over an open flame. If you have a gas hob or can barbecue them, this works well as you get the smoky flavour coming through. Otherwise, place them in the oven at 210°C/190°C Fan/415°F/Gas Mark 6½ for 45 minutes or until the flesh softens. If you are cooking the aubergines over a flame, it will take around 8-10 minutes and you will need to keep turning them using tongs so that the skin is charred evenly. Once they are soft and the sides have shrivelled, remove the aubergines from the heat and place on a plate to cool.

2. Remove the charred skin from the aubergines and run them under water to remove any remaining skin. Place in a bowl and mash using a fork or potato masher.

3. Using a non-stick pan on a medium heat, heat the oil and then add the cumin seeds. Allow them to fizzle in the pan for 15 seconds before adding the green chilli, red onion, ginger and garlic. Move everything around the pan to soften for 6 minutes.

4. Now add the Kashmiri chilli powder, ground turmeric, coriander and salt. Stir well. Add the diced tomatoes and mashed aubergine, then move around the pan for a further 5 minutes.

5. Transfer the spiced aubergine mixture into a serving bowl, scatter the fresh coriander on top and eat warm or at room temperature.

White Cabbage with Fennel Seeds and Sultanas

Preparation time: 15 minutes
Cooking time: 20 minutes
Serves 4-6

2 tbsp vegetable or rapeseed oil

¼ tsp asafoetida powder

I heaped tsp fennel seeds

2 Indian bay leaves/tej patta

I fresh green chilli, sliced lengthways

I large or 2 small potatoes, cut into bite-size pieces

½ large white cabbage, finely shredded (either by hand or using the fine slicer mode on a Magimix)

½ tsp Kashmiri chilli powder

½ tsp ground turmeric

50g sultanas

½ tsp sugar

I tsp salt, or to taste

20ml cold water, if needed

I'm a huge fan of cabbage and I do think it is massively underrated as a vegetable. In the West it's used in slaws, adding crunch and texture, but boiled or steamed it can be a bit bland and unmemorable. In India, spices are added which completely transforms it. I have a couple of cabbage recipes in this book: my South Indian cabbage thoran and this Bengali recipe which was passed down to me by my relatives. Fennel seeds are the key spice and, combined with sultanas, will transform this humble ingredient.

1. In a large wide pan with a lid, warm the oil on a low heat. Even though you are only using half a white cabbage it will produce a lot when shredded, so a pan like a small wok is ideal.

2. When the oil is hot, add the asafoetida, fennel seeds, Indian bay leaves and green chilli. Move them around the pan for 20 seconds before adding the cubed potato.

3. Coat the potato in the spices and keep the pan on a low heat, allowing it to begin to bronze for around 6-8 minutes. Stir intermittently and then place a lid on the pan to help it soften.

4. Rinse the shredded cabbage in a colander under cold running water. Let it drain completely before adding it to the pan. Give everything a good stir and then add the Kashmiri chilli powder, ground turmeric, sultanas, sugar and salt.

5. Cover the pan with a lid and allow the cabbage to soften and cook through, which will take 10 minutes. Make sure you stir occasionally to prevent it sticking to the bottom of the pan.

6. Pierce a potato cube with a sharp knife to see if it has softened sufficiently. If it has not softened enough, add a splash of cold water and place the lid on the pan for a few more minutes. Taste test and check once again before serving.

Avial

Preparation time: 15 minutes
Cooking time: 15 minutes
Serves 4

50g freshly grated or desiccated coconut

1-2 fresh green chillies

½ tsp cumin seeds

2 tbsp coconut oil

2 dried red chillies

1 tsp brown or black mustard seeds

10 curry leaves

150g potato, cut into 4cm (1½ inch) batons

150g carrot, cut into 4cm (1½ inch) batons

150g fine green beans, cut into 4cm (1½ inch) pieces

150g small cauliflower florets

100g peas

1 drumstick/moringa, ends removed, halved and cut into 4cm (1½ inch) pieces (optional)

275ml water

½ tsp ground turmeric

1 tsp salt, or to taste

150ml natural yoghurt

This mild vegetable dish can be found in the southern states of India. It is a great dish to cook if you have a variety of vegetables that need using up in the fridge. Typically in India, drumstick (also known as moringa) is added, along with a combination of four or five of the following: potatoes, gourds, pumpkins, radish, turnip, fine green beans, yams, aubergines, carrots, and peas. There are so many combinations, so do play around and see which ones work best for you.

1. Begin by placing the coconut, green chillies and cumin seeds into a chopper and blitzing roughly. It should not be a smooth paste. Set aside while you proceed with the next steps.

2. Heat the coconut oil in a medium-size deep pan and when hot, add the dried red chillies, mustard seeds and curry leaves. They will immediately begin to sizzle and spit so be careful.

3. Move the spices around the pan for 20 seconds, then add all the vegetables and stir well. Add the water followed by the ground turmeric. Give it a gentle stir and then leave to simmer, with a lid on, for 10 minutes. Check that the vegetables are soft after this time and continue cooking for a few more minutes if needed. If all the vegetables have been cut to a similar size, they should soften around the same time.

4. Add the salt followed by the coconut and chilli paste. Mix in well and then turn the heat down low before adding the natural yoghurt (or coconut milk and water if dairy-free).

5. Simmer gently for a couple more minutes and then check the seasoning before serving.

Notes: To make this dairy-free, add 100ml of coconut milk and 50ml water instead of the natural yoghurt.

FISH AND SEAFOOD

Although Kolkata is not a coastal city, it does lie on the banks of the Hooghly River and has a port. Fish is much loved and eaten throughout the whole of Bengal (which stretches across into Bangladesh) and river fish is particularly prized. I have included some of the recipes that I eat with family in Kolkata in this section but have adapted them with fish that we are more likely to eat in the West. My travels in Kerala have widened my knowledge of the types of fish and shellfish offerings available there too, so they also have a moment to shine in this chapter.

Bengali Mustard Fish Curry

Preparation time: 5 minutes
Cooking time: 15 minutes
Serves 4-6

2 tbsp mustard or vegetable or
rapeseed oil

1 tsp nigella seeds

2-3 fresh green chillies, sliced
lengthways

3 heaped tbsp coarse wholegrain
mustard

2 tsp Dijon mustard

250ml water

1 tsp ground turmeric

1 tsp salt

700g salmon, filleted and skinned

Handful of fresh coriander, roughly
chopped

Fresh lemon or lime wedges, to serve

As a result of having numerous river tributaries flowing through the state of Bengal and out into the Bay of Bengal, Bengalis love fish, particularly freshwater fish. Mustard is celebrated in Bengal and mustard fish curry is a much-loved classic. I tend to make it with filleted salmon, but it also works well with trout or mackerel. In Kolkata, all my relatives love their fish and typically make this curry using freshwater fish such as ilish (hilsa), boal and koi. This is my family's speedy version.

1. Heat a wide shallow pan with a lid and add the oil. Once the oil is hot, bring the heat down to medium-low, then add the nigella seeds and green chillies. These will naturally sizzle away gently in the pan with a tinge of smokiness.

2. After about 20 seconds, add both the mustards and stir them into the pan gently with a wooden spoon. This too will sizzle for a few seconds.

3. Add the water gradually to create a gravy and then add the ground turmeric. Allow to simmer gently for 3 minutes. The flavours from the mustard and nigella are bold and can be a little pungent and smoky. This is to be expected.

4. Add the salt and salmon fillets, then simmer gently with the lid on for 8-10 minutes or until the fish is cooked.

5. Turn the fish over once during the cooking process, gently so as not to break it. Do not overcook the fish nor allow the sauce to dry out. Add a little more water if needed.

6. Sprinkle the curry with fresh coriander and serve immediately with a wedge of lemon or lime on the side for squeezing over.

Bengali Prawn Curry

Preparation time: 10 minutes
Cooking time: 30 minutes
Serves 4

1kg king or tiger prawns, shells on (600g once peeled)

2 tbsp vegetable or rapeseed or mustard oil

1 tsp brown or black mustard seeds

3 Indian bay leaves/tej patta

1 medium-size white onion, finely chopped

1 heaped tsp finely grated garlic or garlic paste

1 heaped tsp finely grated fresh ginger or ginger paste

1 tsp salt

1 tsp Kashmiri chilli powder (less if you are using a different chilli powder)

1 tsp ground cumin

1 tsp ground coriander

1 tsp ground turmeric

1 tsp brown sugar or jaggery

3 medium-size fresh tomatoes, finely chopped or 2 tbsp tinned chopped tomatoes

200ml boiling water

4 tbsp desiccated coconut

1 tsp ground garam masala

This sweet-scented prawn curry, known as chingri maach, is much loved by Bengalis and every household has their own version. My mother-in-law first cooked it for me in my early twenties and it was love at first bite. I like to make it with the large prawns that have the tails still attached; you often find them in the frozen section of Asian grocery stores and at most fishmongers. Otherwise just try to buy the largest prawns you can. In Bengal this dish is traditionally cooked with mustard oil, which is very pungent.

1. First, prepare the prawns by keeping the tails on but removing the heads and shells. Devein them properly on both sides.

2. Heat a tablespoon of the oil in a frying pan or karahi (a traditional circular pan, similar to a wok). On a low heat, seal the prepared prawns so that they turn pink and begin to bronze on both sides, then remove from the pan and set aside. This will take a few minutes on both sides and you may need to do this in batches so the pan isn't crowded.

3. Add a little more oil to the pan if required, then add the mustard seeds and bay leaves. Be careful as the mustard seeds will splutter.

4. After 20 seconds, add the onion, garlic, ginger and salt. Cook gently so that the onion bronzes. This will take around 6-8 minutes.

5. Add the Kashmiri chilli powder, cumin, coriander, turmeric and sugar. Stir them into the onion mixture.

6. Now add the tomatoes and allow them to soften for a couple of minutes before adding the boiling water. Simmer gently for 5 minutes.

7. Return the prawns to the pan and continue to simmer the curry for a further 5 minutes until the prawns are cooked through.

8. Scatter over the desiccated coconut and stir it into the gravy. Simmer for another couple of minutes, then add the ground garam masala and give it a gentle stir just before serving.

Keralan Fish Molee

Preparation time: 15 minutes
Cooking time: 20-25 minutes
Serves 4-6

600g filleted white fish (such as cod, sea bass, sea bream, tilapia)

¾ tsp ground turmeric

½ tsp ground black pepper

½ lemon, juiced

¼ tsp salt

2 tbsp coconut oil

1 tsp brown or black mustard seeds

¼ tsp fenugreek seeds

2 tsp finely grated or chopped fresh ginger, or ginger paste

2 tsp finely grated or chopped garlic, or garlic paste

2-3 fresh green chillies, halved diagonally

15 curry leaves

2 medium white onions, finely chopped

1 tsp salt

1 tsp ground turmeric

1 tsp ground coriander

½ tsp ground black pepper

1 x 400g tin of full-fat coconut milk

50ml water

1 tsp brown sugar or jaggery (optional)

1 large fresh tomato, thinly sliced

Fresh coriander, to serve

Molee (also known as molly or moilee) literally means stew and is commonly found in Keralan cuisine in South India. The fish, or in some cases meat, is stewed in coconut milk and is delicately spiced so as not to overpower the fish. It's quick to prepare and cook and the results are always very pleasing. It's important not to move the fish around too much once it is in the pan as you do not want it breaking up.

1. Chop the fish into approximately 7.5cm (3 inch) pieces. If they are too small they will break up during cooking. Place the fish in a bowl and add the ground turmeric, black pepper, lemon juice and salt. Stir gently, then cover the bowl and leave the fish to marinate for 10 minutes while you prep the rest of the ingredients.

2. Heat the coconut oil in a pan on a low heat. When hot, add the mustard and fenugreek seeds. They will begin to pop immediately so keep them moving around the pan.

3. Stir in the ginger and garlic, followed by the green chillies and curry leaves. Move them around the pan for a minute before adding the chopped onion and salt.

4. Sweat the onions for around 4-5 minutes so that they soften, but do not bronze, and then add the ground turmeric, coriander and black pepper. Mix everything together well.

5. On a low heat, add the thinner part of the coconut milk along with the water and move around the pan. If your coconut milk hasn't separated, just add the whole tin at this point. Simmer on a medium-low heat. Continue to mix well, then cover and simmer for 5 minutes.

6. The coconut gravy will have thickened slightly so now add the fish pieces and simmer. Add the thicker part of the coconut milk (if you have not already added the whole tin) and then turn the heat down. You do not want to boil the creamier coconut milk.

7. Place a lid on the pan and simmer gently for 10 minutes. After 5 minutes, gently stir and cook for the remaining 5 minutes.

8. Add the sugar, then taste the gravy and add more salt or lemon juice if required. Place the sliced tomato on top a few minutes before the cooking time is up. You want the slices to keep their shape and begin to soften but not collapse.

9. Scatter some fresh coriander over the molee just before serving.

Chilli Garlic Mackerel

Preparation time: 15 minutes
Cooking time: 8 minutes
Serves 4

This recipe is a fool-proof approach to cooking fish speedily. Mackerel are stunning fish and have no scales, which makes them very easy to prepare. They do have a punchy flavour and this blend of spices tames the inherent oiliness of the fish. They are a great source of omega 3 and texturally are quite meaty. They barbecue, griddle and pan-fry well, holding their shape and flavour. The preparation is all about getting your hands dirty and working the rub into the fish.

4 mackerel, gutted and cleaned

3 tbsp vegetable or rapeseed oil

2 tsp finely grated garlic or garlic paste

1 tsp freshly ground black pepper

1 tsp chilli flakes, or to taste

½ tsp ground turmeric

1 tsp salt

1 lime, quartered

Notes: You can replace whole mackerel with fillets, but only cook them for 2 minutes on each side.

1. First, clean and gut the mackerel or get your fishmonger to do this for you. Remove the heads and discard. Wash under cold water and then pat dry.

2. Next, make a few shallow incisions on both sides of the mackerel using a fish knife, being careful not to go too deep.

3. Combine 2 tablespoons of the oil with the garlic, spices and salt. Rub this over the fish and into the incisions. Leave to one side for 10 minutes. You can prepare this in advance (a couple of hours would be fine) then cover with cling film and place in the fridge. Bring to room temperature before cooking.

4. Heat a large frying pan or tawa on a high heat and add the remaining vegetable oil. When hot, carefully lay the mackerel in the pan. Leave to cook on one side for 3-4 minutes before flipping over to cook for a further 3-4 minutes. Do not move the fish around during the cooking except for turning it once.

5. Check with a sharp knife that the fish is cooked through sufficiently and leave for a further minute if it requires a little longer. Squeeze a lime wedge over each mackerel and serve immediately.

Turmeric and Nigella Seed Bream Fry

Preparation time: 15 minutes
Cooking time: 15 minutes
Serves 4

This is so simple that it almost seems too easy to include in this book. Sometimes however, the simplest recipes are the best and this one is a firm favourite in my household. The ingredients marry well together, and the actual cooking time is a matter of minutes. If you can't find bream for this recipe, sea bass works equally well.

4 bream fillets, skin on

1 tsp ground turmeric

1 tsp freshly ground black pepper

1 tsp salt

4 tbsp vegetable or rapeseed oil

1 tsp nigella seeds

1 lime, quartered

1. First, place the bream in a bowl and evenly cover with the ground turmeric, black pepper and salt. Cover the bowl with cling film and place in the fridge for 10 minutes before cooking. Bring back to room temperature when you begin the cooking itself.

2. Heat the oil in a frying pan on a medium heat, then add the nigella seeds. They will immediately begin to sizzle in the oil so be careful.

3. Next, add a couple of the bream fillets skin side down first. Do not move them for 3 minutes to allow the skin to crisp evenly. Using a spatula, gently turn them over for a further 3 minutes. Check they are cooked through properly and that the skin is nice and crispy. Turn over again if necessary. Repeat with the remaining sea bream.

4. While the final bream fillets are cooking, place the cooked bream on a plate in a low oven to keep warm.

5. When they are all cooked, serve with a wedge of lime and eat immediately as they will begin to cool quickly. They work well served alongside a kachumber salad (see page 50) and some plain basmati rice.

Prawn Malai Curry

Preparation time: 15 minutes
Cooking time: 25-30 minutes
Serves 4

1kg king or tiger prawns, shells on
(600g once peeled)

½ tsp ground turmeric

½ tsp salt

4 tbsp vegetable or rapeseed oil

2 Indian bay leaves

2 small dried red chillies

4 cloves

4 green cardamom pods, seeds only

5cm (2 inch) cinnamon stick, broken
in two

2 medium white onions, blended to a
smooth paste (approx. 160g)

1 tsp salt, or to taste

1 tsp sugar, or to taste

1 tsp finely grated fresh ginger or ginger
paste

1 tsp finely grated garlic or garlic paste

½ tsp ground turmeric

½ tsp Kashmiri chilli powder (less if
you are using a different chilli powder)

1 x 400ml tin of full-fat coconut milk

1 tbsp tomato purée

150ml water

½ tsp ground garam masala

2 fresh green chillies (optional)

Fresh coriander, to serve

This curry made its way to Kolkata via the Malaysian traders who were undertaking business in the bustling city. The name Malay gradually changed to malai in reference to the creamy coconut milk base of the curry. Typically, I use king prawns for this dish, removing the shells but keeping the tails on. Do keep the discarded shells and heads, then you can make my ginger and lemongrass prawn bisque on page 68 which is a quick and easy meal.

1. First, prepare the prawns by keeping the tails on but removing the heads and shells. Devein them properly on both sides. Place the prepared prawns in a large bowl and rub in the turmeric and salt. Leave to one side for 15 minutes.

2. In a large, deep, wide pan with a lid, heat 3 tablespoons of the oil and cook the marinated prawns in batches for a couple of minutes each, so they are seared and lightly bronzed but not cooked through. Place them on a plate and set aside while you make the gravy.

3. Using the same pan with a little more oil if required, fry the whole spices (bay leaves, dried red chillies, cloves, cardamom seeds and cinnamon stick) for 10 seconds, moving them around the pan.

4. Immediately add the onion paste and move it around the pan. Add the salt and sugar, keep the heat low and keep moving the onion around the pan to help it soften until the raw smell disappears. It will take about 6-8 minutes before it bronzes. Do not rush this part.

5. Now add the ginger and garlic. Move them around the pan for a couple of minutes before adding the ground turmeric and Kashmiri chilli powder.

6. Add about 100ml of the coconut milk to loosen up the contents of the pan, followed by the tomato purée. Mix them in well before adding the remaining coconut milk and water.

7. Simmer the gravy gently with the lid on for a couple of minutes. Return the prawns to the pan and continue to cook for a further 5-7 minutes, by which time the prawns will have cooked through and the gravy will have thickened.

8. In the final minute, sprinkle some ground garam masala on top and add a couple of freshly slit green chillies if you like. Sprinkle the curry with fresh coriander just before serving.

Notes: This curry can also be made with cauliflower, paneer or tofu. Simply follow the steps above, although if you are using cauliflower do not char the green outer leaves. Instead, finely slice them and then add them in Step 7. This curry works equally well with fish like salmon, trout and cod, for example. All you need to do is add the fish in Step 7 and cook it for 7-10 minutes instead of 5-7.

Mussel Molee

Preparation time: 20-30 minutes
Cooking time: 10-12 minutes
Serves 4

45g tamarind pulp (from a block) or
1-2 tsp tamarind paste concentrate

1kg mussels

2 tbsp coconut oil

1 tsp brown or black mustard seeds

15 curry leaves

2 fresh green chillies, halved diagonally
(optional)

1 medium red onion, finely sliced

1 tsp salt

1 heaped tsp finely grated fresh ginger
or ginger paste

1 tsp finely grated garlic or garlic paste

½ tsp ground turmeric

1 x 400g tin of full-fat coconut milk

50ml water

Handful of fresh coriander stalks, finely
chopped or blended with a little water

1 tsp jaggery or brown sugar

Handful of fresh coriander leaves,
chopped

In the UK we are lucky to have plentiful supplies of fresh mussels off our shores, yet the vast majority are exported to our European neighbours. They seem to love them more than we do, but I am convinced that the uninitiated are perhaps intimidated or think they are difficult to cook. This could not be further from the truth. The prep and cleaning can take 10 minutes, but that is as hard as it gets. A molee is a South Indian coconut milk gravy, which works so well with the mussels.

1. If using a block of tamarind, cover the pulp with boiling water in a small bowl. Break it up with the back of a spoon and leave to one side while you prepare the mussels. If you are using tamarind paste concentrate, ignore this step.

2. Place the mussels in a colander in the sink and run cold water over them. Using a scrubbing brush, clean each mussel so all the barnacles and beards, which are fibres that sprout from the shell, are removed. Grab the beard with your thumb and forefinger and move it back and forth; it will release if you give it a little tug. Discard any broken-shelled mussels or ones that do not close. Remember they are sold alive, so if they don't close once you give them a firm tap, then they are already dead and therefore unsafe to eat.

3. Next, heat the coconut oil in a large deep pan with a lid. When hot, add the mustard seeds, curry leaves and green chillies if using, followed by the sliced onion and salt.

4. Allow the onion to soften (but not brown) for 3 minutes, then add the ginger, garlic and ground turmeric. Move around the pan for another minute to remove the raw smell from the garlic.

5. Add the coconut milk and water to the pan, followed by the coriander stalks. Pour the soaked tamarind into a sieve over a bowl and use the back of a spoon to really push the pulp through the sieve. Add the sieved pulp and any liquid in the bowl to the pan, then discard the remaining tamarind stones. If using tamarind paste, add this to the pan instead.

6. Stir in the jaggery or brown sugar and taste test the molee to balance out the flavours. If you are using tamarind paste concentrate you may need a little more than a teaspoon, depending on the brand, so add a little more for extra sourness if you like.

7. Once you are happy with the balance of flavours, add your cleaned mussels. Pour them into the gently boiling molee, give them a good stir and then place a lid on the pan. After 3 minutes, give them a stir again and then replace the lid. Leave for a further 3 minutes. Check to see they have all opened. If they have not opened, leave for another couple of minutes.

8. Scatter the molee with some fresh coriander leaves and then you are ready to serve. If you find any mussels that are unopened, simply discard them.

Speedy Salmon Curry

Preparation time: 10 minutes
Cooking time: 20 minutes
Serves 4

700g salmon fillets, skinned or not as preferred

½ tsp salt

½ tsp ground turmeric

2 tbsp vegetable or rapeseed or mustard oil

1 tsp nigella seeds

1 medium white onion, thinly sliced

1 tsp salt

½ tsp ground turmeric

1 tsp ground coriander

1 tsp ground cumin

½ tsp Kashmiri chilli powder (optional)

2 large ripe tomatoes, finely diced

200-300ml water

1 heaped tsp cornflour or plain flour (optional)

Handful of fresh coriander, to serve

3 fresh green chillies, halved lengthways (optional)

Lemon wedges, to serve

When you are exhausted at the end of the day and can't really be bothered to cook an elaborate meal, yet crave something nourishing with minimal effort, then this speedy salmon curry works wonders. In Bengal, it is referred to as macher jol, macher meaning fish and jol meaning gravy. In Kolkata, it is often made with rui, which is a freshwater fish from the carp family. This recipe is a family favourite and quite typical of those homemade fish curries you find in Kolkata households. You can also substitute the salmon with trout if preferred.

1. Cut the salmon fillets into manageable portions and place into a bowl. Rub the salt and ground turmeric onto the fish and set aside.

2. Heat the oil in a large pan and when hot, add the nigella seeds. They will sizzle once they hit the oil.

3. Move them around the pan for 20 seconds and then immediately add the sliced onion and remaining teaspoon of salt. Fry on a medium heat for 6-8 minutes until lightly bronzed.

4. Now add the following ground spices: turmeric, coriander, cumin and Kashmiri chilli powder. Stir for 20 seconds, then add the tomatoes and stir into the spices. Simmer gently.

5. Add the water and stir well. Place a lid on the pan and simmer for 5 minutes so that the tomatoes soften.

6. To thicken the gravy slightly, place the flour in a bowl and add 2 tablespoons of cold water. Stir until smooth and then add this paste to the gravy.

7. Gently place the salmon pieces into the pan (with the skin facing upwards, if you have kept the skin on) and simmer for 7 minutes with the lid on the pan.

8. Use a spoon to gently turn the salmon pieces over and add a little more water if necessary. It will only need a couple more minutes.

9. If you prefer a thicker sauce, add less water and vice versa. It's not an exact science and more down to personal taste.

10. Serve the curry with a scattering of fresh coriander, a couple of green chillies if you fancy and some lemon wedges for squeezing over.

Squid Coconut Fry

Preparation time: 15 minutes
Cooking time: 8-10 minutes
Serves 2, or 4 alongside other dishes

2 tbsp coconut oil

½ tsp brown or black mustard seeds

2 small dried red chillies or fresh green chillies, halved

10 pieces of thinly sliced fresh or dried coconut

3 cloves of garlic, thinly sliced

1 tsp finely grated fresh ginger

1 fresh green chilli, sliced lengthways

10 curry leaves

1 small red onion, finely chopped

½ tsp salt

½ tsp Kashmiri chilli powder

½ tsp ground coriander

½ tsp ground turmeric

300g squid tubes, chopped into thin rings

1 tbsp lemon juice

¼ tsp freshly ground black pepper

¼ tsp ground garam masala

This Keralan squid dish is cooked in minutes and is best eaten straight away. You can prepare it with either small or larger squid rings. The taste evokes happy memories of my travels in Kerala, on the coast with the palm trees, white sand beaches and the warm breeze coming off the Arabian sea. If you don't want to gut the squid yourself, ask your fishmonger to prepare it for you and cut it into thin rings. I particularly love to cook this dish with the smaller squid.

1. First, prepare all the ingredients and have everything to hand, because the dish takes no time to cook and you will want to eat it immediately. This dish is not good reheated.

2. Heat the coconut oil in a wide shallow pan or frying pan. When hot, add the mustard seeds and chillies. Move them around the pan for 10 seconds before adding the thin coconut slices. Keep the pan on a medium-low heat, as the mustard seeds will splutter.

3. After 20 seconds, add the garlic, ginger, green chilli and curry leaves. Move everything around the pan for a minute, then stir in the finely chopped red onion and salt. Mix well.

4. Now add the ground spices: Kashmiri chilli powder, coriander and turmeric. Allow the flavours to come together in the pan and the onion to soften for 3-5 minutes.

5. Stir the squid rings into the onion and spices. Gently cook for a further 3 minutes.

6. Finally, add the lemon juice, freshly ground black pepper and garam masala, stirring gently.

7. Serve immediately. All the wonderful flavours will have wrapped themselves around the squid, culminating in the most appetising of dishes.

Tamarind Prawn Curry

Preparation time: 20 minutes + 30 minutes marinating
Cooking time: 30 minutes
Serves 4-6

1kg king or tiger prawns, shells on (600g once peeled)

½ tsp salt

½ tsp ground turmeric

½ tsp Kashmiri chilli powder (less if you are using a different chilli powder)

1 heaped tsp ground coriander

50g tamarind pulp (from a block) or 2 tsp tamarind paste concentrate

300ml boiling water

4 tbsp vegetable or rapeseed oil

1 tsp brown or black mustard seeds

½ tsp fenugreek seeds

10-15 curry leaves

2-3 fresh green chillies, sliced diagonally

2 medium red onions, finely chopped

1 tsp salt, or to taste

2 tsp finely grated fresh ginger or ginger paste

2 tsp finely grated garlic or garlic paste

1 tsp ground turmeric

1 tsp Kashmiri chilli powder (less if you are using a different chilli powder)

2 large tomatoes, finely chopped

1 tsp light brown sugar or jaggery

Notes: You can also make this curry with fish: salmon, trout or cod would work well. Instead of searing, add them at the very end and simmer them in the gravy for around 7-10 minutes, turning them over once if you can.

Zingy and deliciously spicy, this South Indian prawn curry can be enjoyed by the whole family. It is worth buying tamarind in a block for this curry, instead of a paste. It requires soaking for 10-15 minutes and then sieving, so minimal effort for memorable results. I also recommend buying any large prawns of your choice with the shells on and then prepping them yourself so that you can keep the shells and heads to make my ginger and lemongrass bisque (see page 68). Smaller prawns which have been deshelled will also be delicious.

1. First, prepare the prawns by keeping the tails on but removing the heads and shells. Devein them properly on both sides.

2. Place the prawns in a large bowl and then add the salt, turmeric, Kashmiri chilli powder and coriander. Mix well and leave to one side for 30 minutes.

3. Meanwhile, place the tamarind in a small bowl and cover with the boiling water. Break up the block as much possible with a spoon and leave for 10-15 minutes. If you are using tamarind paste, skip this step.

4. Heat 2 tablespoons of the oil in a frying pan on a medium heat. When hot, add some of the prawns. You do not want to overcrowd the pan, so I suggest doing this in a couple of batches. Bronze both sides, which will take about 2 minutes in total. Transfer the seared prawns to a plate lined with kitchen roll as you do the rest.

5. In a medium-size wide pan with a lid, heat up the rest of the oil. Add the mustard seeds and fenugreek seeds followed by the curry leaves and green chillies. Move them around the pan for 10 seconds and then add the onions and salt, turning the heat down.

6. Allow the onion to completely soften and begin to bronze. This will take around 6-8 minutes. Next, fold the ginger and garlic pastes into the onions. After another few minutes, add the ground turmeric and Kashmiri chilli powder followed by the tomatoes.

7. Meanwhile, drain the soaked tamarind in a sieve over a bowl and use the back of a spoon to push all the goodness through. Discard the tamarind stones left in the sieve.

8. Add the tamarind liquid in the bowl (you should have about 300ml) to the pan along with the brown sugar or jaggery and simmer for a few minutes. If you are using tamarind paste concentrate, add it now along with 300ml of warm water.

9. Return the prawns to the pan and stir to cover them with the tamarind gravy. Place a lid on the pan and simmer at a gentle bubble on a low heat for 8 minutes. Add more water if it begins to look dry. Taste test after this time to check on the salt and sour notes, then serve.

MEAT

This chapter includes some showstopping recipes, but as you will see they are mainly chicken and lamb curries, with just one pork dish. You will also find a chicken liver curry, which I promise is nothing like the dreadful liver that haunted so many childhoods in this country. It is a great dish so I hope that many of you will try it. You will notice there are no beef curries. I rarely eat beef these days so wanted to show you the curries that I cook, that work and that you and your family and friends will love. For those who are vegetarian and vegan, please follow these recipes and simply substitute the meat with paneer, tofu or cauliflower. Fry them lightly in a little oil first to bronze before adding them to the gravy later.

Bengali Lamb Chop Curry

Preparation time: 15 minutes (includes making the masala)
Cooking time: 1 hour - 1 hour 15 minutes
Serves 4

2 tbsp mustard or vegetable or rapeseed oil

1 tsp panch phoron/Bengali five spice

2 Indian bay leaves

5cm (2 inch) cinnamon stick, broken in two

4 green cardamom pods

1 black cardamom pod

4 cloves

1 large red onion, thinly sliced

1 tsp salt

3 cloves of garlic, roughly chopped

1 tsp finely grated fresh ginger or ginger paste

3 tomatoes, roughly chopped

1-2 fresh green chillies

8 lamb chops

½ tsp Kashmiri chilli powder

1 tsp ground turmeric

1 heaped tsp North Indian meat masala powder (see page 218)

750ml water

Fresh coriander, to serve

This deliciously warming and earthy curry includes the Bengali five spice known as panch phoron, which is unique to the Indian state of Bengal. It also includes a teaspoon of my North Indian meat masala, giving it extra layers of flavour and depth. It's a favourite among my cookery class recipes and always receives a very positive reception. I hope you agree.

1. First prepare the North Indian meat masala powder on page 218.

2. Heat the oil in a deep cast iron pan. Add the panch phoron, bay leaves, cinnamon stick, green and black cardamom and cloves.

3. Move the spices around the pan for a minute before adding the onion and salt. Keep on a low heat and gently bronze the onion, which will take 6-8 minutes.

4. Add the garlic and ginger, then add the chopped tomatoes and green chillies. Simmer for a further few minutes before adding the lamb chops.

5. Stir all the ground spices into the pan, including the North Indian meat masala, and mix well. Let this simmer for a couple of minutes before adding the water. It will seem like quite a lot of liquid, but this will thicken and reduce to virtually nothing over the course of 1 hour to 1 hour and 15 minutes, after which time you'll end up with a delicious, unctuous curry.

6. Gently simmer on a medium heat, with the lid on, stirring intermittently during the cooking time. Taste test to check the salt levels. If you find there is still a lot of liquid, keep it simmering until you have a deliciously thick gravy.

7. Serve the curry with a scattering of fresh coriander.

Chettinad Pepper Chicken

Preparation time: 15 minutes
Cooking time: 1 hour 10 minutes
Serves 4-6

This much-loved South Indian curry originates from the state of Tamil Nadu and the region of Chettinad. It is a dry curry which is deliciously hot, not from chilli but from peppery heat. The spices dance on your tongue in a pleasingly addictive way. Definitely not a curry for the faint hearted.

For the masala powder

3 tsp black peppercorns

2 tsp coriander seeds

2 tsp fennel seeds

2 tsp cumin seeds

For the curry

1kg chicken thighs, cut into bite-size pieces (or 1 whole chicken, skinned and cut into 10-12 pieces)

1 tsp ground turmeric

½ tsp Kashmiri chilli powder

3 tbsp coconut oil

5 cardamom pods, opened

7.5cm (3 inches) cinnamon stick or bark

10-15 curry leaves

1 tsp brown or black mustard seeds

2 white onions, finely chopped

1 tsp salt, or to taste

3 tsp ginger-garlic paste (see page 220)

2-3 large tomatoes, finely chopped

25ml water

Fresh coriander leaves, to serve

1. Start by warming a frying pan. When hot, add the masala powder ingredients and move them around the pan for a minute. You will start to smell their wonderful aromas but be careful not to let them burn. Take the pan off the heat and once cooled, blend the toasted spices in your spice grinder or grind in a pestle and mortar to a smooth powder.

2. Next, place the chicken pieces in a bowl with the ground turmeric and Kashmiri chilli powder. If you don't have Kashmiri chilli powder, regular chilli powder is fine, although it will be hotter so use a little less. Leave the chicken to marinate while you start cooking.

3. Heat the coconut oil in a large deep pan, then add the cardamom pods, cinnamon stick or bark, curry leaves and mustard seeds. Be careful as they will splutter in the hot oil.

4. Add the onions to the pan and keep the heat low while they begin to bronze. Add a little salt at this stage to speed up the process. This will take around 8 minutes.

5. Add the ginger-garlic paste to the pan and stir in thoroughly. After a couple of minutes, add the tomatoes. Let them soften completely over the next 3-4 minutes.

6. Now add the spiced chicken pieces to the pan and coat with all the ingredients. Add the freshly ground masala powder to the pan and stir into the chicken mixture. Add the water and place a lid on the pan. More liquid will naturally be released over the course of the cooking, so do not add any more. Stir intermittently for the next 40-50 minutes (cooking meat on the bone will require closer to 50 minutes).

7. Taste test and add more salt if required, then leave the dish to rest before serving, allowing the flavours to infuse and relax. Top with a scattering of fresh coriander when ready to eat.

Notes: If you are cooking this dish in advance, allow it to cool completely before placing in the fridge. Remove from the fridge an hour before eating, and then gently warm up.

Chicken Liver Curry

Preparation time: 15 minutes
Cooking time: 25-30 minutes
Serves 4-6

4 tbsp vegetable or rapeseed oil

1 large potato, peeled and diced into 2.5cm cubes

1 large white onion, finely chopped

1 tsp salt

2 fresh red or green chillies, sliced lengthways (optional)

1 heaped tsp finely grated fresh ginger or ginger paste

500g chicken livers, chopped into bite-size pieces

1 tsp ground turmeric

1 tsp ground cumin

1 tsp ground coriander

1 small cinnamon stick

3 green cardamom pods, opened

5 cloves of garlic, kept whole

100ml water

Fresh coriander, to serve

I cannot stress enough how good this curry is. Anyone who has grown up in the UK (especially during the 80s) has a deep distrust of offal, largely stemming from school dinners which made liver taste bland and uninteresting. Cooked with spices, however, it transforms into something magnificent. Chicken livers are affordable and packed with iron, vitamin B12 and protein. My Bengali in-laws first made this for me, and I was surprised by how addictively good it tasted. Be brave. Try it. I think it might just change your view on chicken livers if it wasn't already positive!

1. Heat half the oil in a large deep pan, add the potato and gently fry for 5 minutes, stirring so that the cubes don't stick to the bottom of the pan.

2. Remove the potatoes with a slotted spoon and place in a bowl. Using the same pan, add the rest of the oil, if required, to fry the onion with the salt until it begins to bronze. This will take around 6-8 minutes.

3. Add the green or red chillies (if using) and grated ginger, stirring them into the onions. After 2 minutes, add the chicken livers and move around the pan for 5 minutes, so that they seal and lighten in colour.

4. Add the ground spices along with the cinnamon stick, green cardamom, garlic cloves and fried potato.

5. Move everything around the pan until well mixed, then add 50ml of the water and stir in gently. If required, add the final 50ml to help soften the potato and garlic. Place a lid on the pan and simmer gently for 15 minutes.

6. Check on the seasoning and add more salt if required. When the curry is cooked, sprinkle over some fresh coriander and serve.

Chicken Methi Malai

**Preparation time: 10 minutes + 30
minutes marinating
Cooking time: 50 minutes
Serves 4-6**

1kg boneless chicken thighs, chopped
into 4 pieces each

For the marinade

½ tsp salt

½ tsp Kashmiri chilli powder

½ tsp ground turmeric

½ tsp ground coriander

1 lemon, juice only

1 tbsp ginger-garlic paste (see page
220)

For the curry

2 tbsp vegetable or rapeseed oil

6 cloves

5 black peppercorns

3 black cardamom pods

2 medium white onions, finely diced

1-2 fresh green chillies, finely chopped

1 tsp salt

1 tbsp ginger-garlic paste

1 tsp ground turmeric

1 tsp ground coriander

1 tsp Kashmiri chilli powder

150g natural yoghurt

3 heaped tbsp dried fenugreek leaves

150g cream

50ml water

This fragrant curry is always a crowd pleaser. The dried fenugreek leaves add a wonderful earthy taste that works so well with the chicken. They are also known as kasoori methi and not generally a familiar ingredient in Western cooking. They were a revelation when I first started using them. You need to crumble them, using your hands, into the curry to release their strong yet sweet aroma. This dish works equally well if you want to make it vegetarian by replacing the chicken with 500g of paneer.

1. Place the chicken pieces into a large bowl, add the ingredients for the marinade, turn until the chicken is coated and then cover for 30 minutes. If you are making this with paneer, simply cube it and then fry gently in a frying pan for 5 minutes so that one or two sides are bronzed. Remove with a slotted spoon and then continue with the next steps.

2. For the curry, heat the oil in a large, deep pan and then add the whole spices: cloves, black peppercorns and black cardamom.

3. Fry the spices for 20 seconds and then add the onion, green chilli and salt. Move everything around the pan for 6-8 minutes, allowing the onion to soften and bronze, before adding the ginger-garlic paste. Continue to move this around the pan for a couple of minutes.

4. Now add the ground turmeric, ground coriander and Kashmiri chilli powder, stirring them in thoroughly. Turn the heat down and add the natural yoghurt, followed by the dried fenugreek leaves.

5. Place the marinated chicken (or paneer if using) in the pan, coating all the pieces in the spices and yoghurt, then pour in the cream and half the water.

6. Simmer gently on a low heat, turning the chicken intermittently for the next 40 minutes. Place a lid on the pan during this period. Add the rest of the water to loosen if required (you may find this is unnecessary). This curry does have quite a lot of gravy, as water will be released from the chicken itself. Cook it for a little longer with the lid off if you prefer the gravy to reduce.

7. Taste test the curry before serving to check the salt levels and add a little more if required.

Fenugreek Lamb Curry

Preparation time: 15 minutes
Cooking time: 1 hour 10 minutes
Serves 4-6

2 tbsp vegetable or rapeseed oil

2 large white onions, finely chopped

1 tsp salt

2 tsp finely grated garlic or garlic paste

2 tsp finely grated fresh ginger or ginger paste

2 fresh green chillies, sliced lengthways

1.3kg lamb neck or shoulder, cut into bite-size pieces

1 tsp ground turmeric

2 tsp ground cumin

2 tsp ground coriander

1 tsp Kashmiri chilli powder

2 tsp North Indian meat masala powder (see page 218)

2 large tomatoes, finely chopped

200ml water

250ml yoghurt

1 tbsp lemon juice

1 large bunch of fresh fenugreek leaves (approx. 70g) or 6 tbsp dried fenugreek leaves

The leaves and seeds of fenugreek, or methi as it is known in India, are common in Indian cooking. You need to use the golden-brown seeds sparingly, as too many can make the dish bitter. The green leaves – dried and fresh – add a wonderful earthy, nutty aroma to the dish, quite unlike any other flavour in the Western pantry. In India, meat curries and dals are cooked in the pressure cooker, but as this is not common in the West, I've cooked this and all my curries in this book in my cast iron pan and kadai, which looks like a small wok.

1. First prepare the North Indian meat masala powder on page 218.

2. Heat the oil in a large cast iron or other deep, wide pan preferably with a lid. When hot, add the finely chopped onion and salt. Allow the onion to soften and lightly bronze over the next 6-8 minutes.

3. Next add the garlic and ginger, moving them around the pan for a few minutes to remove the raw smell before adding the green chillies and diced lamb.

4. Stir in all the ground spices along with the Kashmiri chilli and masala powders. Mix well before adding the chopped tomatoes and water. Place a lid on the pan and simmer gently for 10 minutes.

5. Whisk the yoghurt until smooth and then stir this into the curry, followed by the lemon juice. Finally, add the fenugreek leaves and stir them into the curry.

6. Cook on a low heat for 50 minutes, stirring intermittently, until the lamb is soft and tender. When done, check the seasoning and add more salt as required before serving.

Goan Pork Vindaloo

Preparation time: 30 minutes + optional marinating time
Cooking time: I hour
Serves 6

For the spice masala

I tsp black peppercorns

2 tsp black mustard seeds

2 tsp cumin seeds

3 tsp coriander seeds

6 cloves

7.5cm (3 inches) cinnamon stick or bark

For the paste

10 dried Kashmiri chillies

20g fresh ginger

5 cloves of garlic

4 tbsp white vinegar

For the curry

1.4kg pork, cut into 2cm cubes (I use half shoulder, half belly)

I tsp salt

I tsp brown sugar or jaggery

50g tamarind pulp (from a block) or 2 tsp tamarind paste

100ml hot water

2 tbsp vegetable or rapeseed oil

2 large white onions, thinly sliced into half moons

15 curry leaves

½ tsp ground turmeric

10 very thin batons of fresh ginger, to serve

The Portuguese ruled Goa for 450 years, so it is understandable that the local cuisine was heavily influenced by the colonisers. Vindaloo itself derives from the Portuguese dish 'carne de vinha d'alhos' meaning 'meat with wine and garlic', but the locals made their own interpretation of the dish by replacing the wine with vinegar and adding chillies. It's a classic which is loved the world over. I opt for dried Kashmiri chillies here, which are not as hot as some, so if you use another variety, I recommend using slightly fewer, unless you really love chilli heat.

1. Begin by heating a frying pan and dry frying all the ingredients for the spice masala. Move them around the pan to release their wonderful aromas, which will take around I minute. Transfer the toasted spices to a bowl and leave to cool before using a spice grinder or pestle and mortar to grind them into a smooth powder.

2. For the paste, first soak the dried chillies (using fewer if they are a different variety) in warm water for 10 minutes and then remove the stems. Meanwhile, peel and roughly chop the ginger and garlic, then blend it with the soaked chillies and vinegar to form a smooth paste.

3. For the curry itself, place the cubed pork into a large bowl and add the salt, brown sugar or jaggery, spice masala and chilli paste. Use your hands to thoroughly mix it all together.

4. Cover the bowl with cling film and ideally place it in the fridge for an hour or longer if you can (overnight is ideal) and then bring the marinated pork back to room temperature before cooking. However, if you are pressed for time simply continue with the next steps.

5. Place the tamarind pulp in a small bowl and cover with the hot water. Break it up a little with the back of a spoon, then leave to soak for 10 minutes. Pour the soaked tamarind into a sieve over a bowl and use the spoon to push the pulp through, leaving the stones in the sieve. Discard these and place the strained tamarind juice and pulp to one side.

6. Heat the oil in a large deep cast-iron pan, then add the sliced onion, curry leaves and turmeric. Allow the onion to soften while stirring, which will take around 6-8 minutes.

7. Add the pork along with the tamarind mixture (if you are using paste, add it now) and then simmer gently on a low heat for I hour, stirring intermittently.

8. After this time, taste the gravy and add more salt if necessary. Leave the vindaloo to rest before serving, then top with the fresh ginger batons before eating.

Notes: You can cook this curry ahead of time, even the day before you plan to eat it. Place it in the fridge once it has cooled if you plan to eat it later in the day. Always bring to room temperature before reheating the curry.

Homestyle Bengali Chicken Curry

Preparation time: 15 minutes
Cooking time: 40 minutes
Serves 4-6

3 tbsp vegetable or rapeseed oil

4 cloves

5 green cardamom pods,
opened slightly

2 x 5cm (2 inch) cinnamon sticks

2 Indian bay leaves

1 large white onion, roughly chopped

2 tsp finely grated fresh ginger or ginger
paste

3 heaped tbsp tinned chopped
tomatoes or 2 large fresh tomatoes,
diced

1kg (10-12) chicken thighs, skinned
and chopped into bite-size pieces if
boneless

1 tsp each ground turmeric, cumin and
coriander

1 tsp Kashmiri chilli powder

1-2 tsp salt, to taste

6 cloves of garlic, kept whole

3 medium potatoes, halved or
quartered

2 large carrots, chopped into chunks

2 fresh green chillies, sliced lengthways
or finely chopped (optional)

200ml water

½ tsp ground garam masala

Fresh coriander, to serve

Lemon wedges, to serve

Every Bengali household has their own chicken curry recipe. I was taught this one by family members in my twenties. It has become a family favourite that brings comfort and joy every time we eat it. Typically, we cook this on the bone, often carving a whole chicken into 10-12 pieces and removing the skin. It works equally well with chicken thighs on or off the bone. I have suggested the boneless route for the recipe below, but it is up to you. Whole spices are used instead of a powdered spice masala, which is very common with Bengali cuisine.

1. Heat the oil in a large, deep, cast iron pot. When hot, add the whole spices: the cloves, green cardamom pods, cinnamon sticks and Indian bay leaves. Move them around in the oil to release the aromas for a minute, then add the onion with a pinch of salt to help it soften.

2. Keep the heat on low-medium so that the onion becomes translucent, soft and bronzed. This should take around 8-10 minutes.

3. Add the ginger and move around the pan for a couple of minutes, then stir in the tomatoes (I often just used tinned for this recipe) and mix well with the ginger, onion and spices. Simmer gently for a few more minutes.

4. Now add your chicken pieces and fold them into the tomato-onion gravy. Add all the ground spices, Kashmiri chilli powder and salt followed by the garlic cloves, potatoes and carrots. Stir everything well so that chicken and vegetables are completely coated in the spiced gravy. If you would like some extra heat, add the green chillies now, but this is optional.

5. On a medium heat, allow the curry to cook through, stirring at intervals. Add the water to create a looser gravy. Water will also be released by the chicken itself as it cooks. You can always add more water during the cooking process if you feel the dish requires it.

6. After 30-40 minutes the curry should be completely cooked. Use a knife to make sure the carrots and potatoes are soft. If they remain hard, add a little more water into the gravy and cook for another 10 minutes.

7. Sprinkle the curry with a little garam masala at the very end and serve with a scattering of fresh coriander and some lemon wedges on the side.

Keralan Coconut Chicken Curry

Preparation time: 15 minutes
Cooking time: 50 minutes - 1 hour
Serves 4-6

2 tbsp coconut oil

½ tsp whole black peppercorns

1 tsp brown or black mustard seeds

4 x 5cm (2 inch) cinnamon sticks or bark

5 green cardamom pods, opened

7 dried Kashmiri chillies

10-15 curry leaves

10 cloves

1 star anise

1 tsp salt, or to taste

2 medium red onions, finely diced

2.5cm (1 inch) fresh ginger, finely sliced into batons

3 cloves of garlic, finely diced

1kg boneless chicken thighs, cut into bite-size pieces

1 x 400ml tin of full-fat coconut milk

2 medium potatoes, quartered

160ml coconut cream (optional)

1 tsp ground black pepper

¼ tsp ground garam masala

An hour out of Kochi, in the lush Keralan countryside, is the house of Moly and Lieutenant Colonel Mathens and their son Philip. Many years ago, my family and I spent the day with them all, admiring all the spices growing in their garden and cooking alongside Moly in her kitchen. We cooked so many delicious recipes, but this is the one I remember the most clearly. It has hints of spice that play on your tongue without overpowering the whole dish.

1. In a deep pan – cast iron works well – add the coconut oil. When hot, add all the whole spices (peppercorns, mustard seeds, cinnamon sticks, cardamom pods, dried chillies, curry leaves, cloves, star anise) and move them around the pan for 20 seconds before adding the salt and diced onion.

2. Leave this mixture to cook for 5 minutes so that the onion softens and the raw smell dissipates. Add the ginger and garlic and cook gently for a further 2-3 minutes on a medium-low heat.

3. Now add the chicken and stir for a couple of minutes before adding the tin of coconut milk. In Kerala, typically you add the thin coconut milk at this point and the thicker creamier part later on. I realise this is hard to achieve with some brands of coconut milk so you can just add the whole tin at this stage.

4. Simmer the curry for 20 minutes and then add the potatoes and give it a good stir. Let the chicken and potato simmer on a medium-low heat. After 15 minutes, use a sharp knife to check if the potato has softened sufficiently and the chicken is cooked through. If it needs a little longer, keep it simmering for an extra 10-15 minutes. If you are using chicken on the bone, it will require about 40-50 minutes of cooking time in total.

5. At the very end of the cooking time, turn the heat down very low and add the coconut cream if using. Do not let it boil or it will split.

6. Add the ground black pepper and garam masala. Taste the curry to check the salt levels and add a little more if required before serving.

Notes: You can also cook this on the bone with chicken thighs or by using a whole chicken, skinned and chopped into 10-12 pieces.

Kosha Mangsho

**Preparation time: 15 minutes +
marinating time
Cooking time: 1 hour 40 minutes
Serves 6**

1.3kg lamb neck or shoulder, cut into
2.5cm cubes

100g plain yoghurt

1 tsp ground turmeric

1 tbsp white wine vinegar

4 tbsp vegetable or rapeseed or
mustard oil

4 cloves

3 Indian bay leaves

3 dried red chillies

2 black cardamom pods

6 green cardamom pods

5cm (2 inch) cinnamon stick

2 large white onions, finely sliced

3 tsp finely grated garlic or garlic paste

3 tsp finely grated fresh ginger or ginger
paste

1-2 tsp salt, to taste

2 heaped tsp ground cumin

1 heaped tsp ground coriander

1 tsp Kashmiri chilli powder

200ml hot water

3 medium potatoes, peeled and halved
or quartered

1 tsp ground garam masala

1 tsp ghee, to serve (optional)

Mention the words kosha mangsho – lamb curry – to a Bengali and you'll see their spirits lifted and smiles across their faces. It's a special occasion curry that is on every wedding and family ceremony's menu. Kosha means dry, but not in the Western sense, as it still has a gravy. In Kolkata, my relatives cook this in a pressure cooker, but I cook it on the stove top, which takes a little longer but still works well. Typically, it is cooked using mustard oil, but as that's not so readily available in the UK, vegetable or rapeseed will work equally well.

1. Place the lamb in a large bowl with the yoghurt, ground turmeric and vinegar. Cover the bowl, place it in the fridge and leave the lamb to marinate for an hour or longer, even overnight if you have time. After marinating, bring the lamb to room temperature.

2. In a large, deep pan – ideally cast iron – add the oil and when hot, add the cloves, bay leaves, dried red chillies, black and green cardamom and cinnamon.

3. Move the spices around the pan for 20 seconds; the aromas will immediately be released. Add the finely sliced onions and fry on a medium heat for 8-10 minutes, until they become a golden-brown colour. You do not want to rush this part as it will really add depth of flavour if they are bronzed nicely.

4. Add the garlic and ginger and move around the pan for 3 minutes before adding the marinated lamb along with a teaspoon of the salt. Allow the mixture to simmer for 10 minutes so that the meat browns, stirring intermittently so that it does not catch on the bottom of the pan.

5. Add the ground cumin, coriander and Kashmiri chilli powder to the pan and stir in well. Pour in half the hot water, stir again and then cover with a lid.

6. Cook the curry on a medium-low heat for 1 hour 30 minutes. After 40 minutes, add the remaining water along with the potatoes. If you put these in too early, they will disintegrate.

7. Once the total cooking time is up, the meat should be soft and tender and the potatoes nicely soft. If the mixture becomes too dry during the cooking process, simply add a little more hot water.

8. Just before serving, add the garam masala and mix in well. Check the salt levels and add the remaining teaspoon if required, then stir and simmer for a couple more minutes before serving. If you want to be authentic, add a dollop of ghee on top for extra decadence.

Lamb Keema

Preparation time: 15 minutes
Cooking time: 30 minutes
Serves 4

2 tbsp vegetable or rapeseed oil

1 tsp cumin seeds

3 cloves

2 Indian bay leaves/tej patta (optional)

4 green cardamom pods, opened

1-2 fresh green chillies, finely chopped

1 large white onion, finely chopped

1 tsp salt, or to taste

1 heaped tsp finely grated fresh ginger or ginger paste

2 tsp finely grated garlic or garlic paste

800g lamb mince

1 tsp ground turmeric

2 tsp ground coriander

½ tsp Kashmiri chilli powder

2 medium tomatoes, finely diced

150g frozen peas

1 tsp ground garam masala

Growing up in the UK, shepherd's pie and lasagne were, and still are, staple family meals. Keema is the Indian version and my family absolutely love it. This mince dish is more akin to traditional pasta sauces, but with the addition of warming spices it gives a gentle nod to the Indian subcontinent. I love to make this with lamb, but you can make it with beef or plant-based alternatives if you want to go down the vegan route. To bulk out the recipe, add a few boiled and quartered potatoes 5 minutes after you add the mince.

1. Heat the oil in a pan on a medium heat and when hot, add the cumin seeds which will immediately begin to sizzle.

2. Follow this by adding the cloves, Indian bay leaves, cardamom pods and green chillies. Move everything around the pan for 20 seconds before adding the onion and salt.

3. Keep the heat low and allow the onion to soften and begin to bronze. This will take around 6-8 minutes. Continue to move the onion around the pan so that it does not catch on the bottom and burn.

4. Now add the ginger and garlic and stir them into the onion. After 2 minutes, add the lamb mince and use the back of a wooden spoon to break it up.

5. Move the mince around the pan for 3-4 minutes before adding the ground spices and Kashmiri chilli powder.

6. Once the meat has changed colour from pink to brown, add the tomatoes and frozen peas. Stir them into the mince and then simmer it on a low heat for 15 minutes, continuing to stir intermittently.

7. Taste to check the salt levels and then finally add the garam masala. Stir it into the keema and serve with basmati rice or any of the Indian flatbreads in this book.

Lamb Rogan Josh

Preparation time: 15 minutes
Cooking time: 1 hour 30 minutes
Serves 4

6 tbsp vegetable or rapeseed oil

1kg lamb neck fillet, cut into bite-size pieces

1 heaped tsp fennel seeds

1 tsp cumin seeds

2 Indian bay leaves

4 cloves

6 green cardamom pods, seeds only

7.5cm (3 inches) cinnamon stick or bark

2-3 white onions, finely chopped

2 tsp finely grated garlic or garlic paste

2 tsp finely grated fresh ginger or ginger paste

1 tsp salt, or to taste

1 tsp paprika

2 tsp ground coriander

½ tsp Kashmiri chilli powder (less if you are using a different chilli powder)

5 medium-size tomatoes, finely diced

1 tsp tomato purée

600ml vegetable stock

3 tbsp yoghurt (optional)

Fresh coriander leaves, to serve

This aromatic North Indian lamb curry was introduced to Kashmir by the Mughals and remains hugely popular. Made with either lamb or goat, it contains warming spices which are flavoursome, but not hot. Traditionally dried cockscomb flower, known as amaranth, combined with a little Kashmiri chilli powder, gave the dish a deep red colour. As amaranth is hard to source, my version uses a little paprika combined with Kashmiri chilli powder that works well as a substitute. It is great cooked in advance and then placed in the fridge once cooled.

1. Heat a large deep casserole pan and add 3 tablespoons of the oil. When hot, add the lamb and allow it to bronze on all sides, which will take around 10 minutes. Remove with a slotted spoon and place in a large bowl. Reserve the juices from the pan.

2. Add the remaining oil to the same pan. When the oil is hot, keep the pan on a medium heat, add the fennel and cumin seeds, Indian bay leaves, cloves, cardamom seeds and cinnamon. Move everything around the pan for 20 seconds, then add the onion and cook until it turns light brown. This will take between 6-8 minutes.

3. Now stir in the garlic and ginger, move them around the pan for a couple of minutes, then add the salt, paprika, ground coriander and Kashmiri chilli powder.

4. Stir the spices well before adding the fresh tomatoes and tomato purée. Allow the fresh tomatoes to soften for a couple of minutes before returning the lamb to the pan. Coat the lamb in the spices and then add the vegetable stock along with any reserved lamb juices.

5. Bring the contents of the pan to boiling point and then reduce the heat to medium. Cook for 1 hour with the lid off, stirring at intervals. You may find you need to let it cook for a further 10-15 minutes if the gravy has not reduced enough after this time.

6. Taste to check the salt level and add more if necessary. If you like, you can also stir some yoghurt through the curry at the end, but this is only optional.

7. Scatter the rogan josh with some fresh coriander leaves and serve with naan bread (see page 178).

Notes: If you are making this in advance, keep it in the fridge and bring to room temperature before reheating. It also freezes well.

Opium Chicken

**Preparation time: 30 minutes +
marinating time
Cooking time: 40 minutes
Serves 4-6**

1kg boneless chicken thighs, cut into
bite-size pieces

For the marinade

2 tbsp lemon juice

2 tsp mustard or vegetable oil

2 tsp finely grated fresh ginger or ginger
paste

2 tsp finely grated garlic or garlic paste

¼ tsp ground turmeric

For the curry

2 tbsp vegetable or rapeseed oil

4 green cardamom pods

4 cloves

2 bay leaves

2.5cm (1 inch) cinnamon stick

1 tsp cumin seeds

1 tsp fennel seeds

2 white onions, finely diced

1 tsp salt

6 tbsp (65g) white poppy seeds

200ml water

4 fresh green chillies, sliced lengthways

½ tsp brown sugar or jaggery

Fresh coriander, to serve

Bengal was at the heart of opium cultivation and production during the 19th century, run by the East India company. It was not surprising that the use of poppy seeds found its way into the local cuisine, with aloo posto – potato and poppy seeds – becoming a delicacy that remains popular. The other much loved poppy seed dish is to combine posto – white poppy seed – with succulent chicken (murghi) and fresh green chillies. You create a paste that becomes a gravy that coats the chicken, to be eaten with some bhat (steamed rice) and dal.

1. Start by coating the chicken pieces in all the marinade ingredients. Cover and leave to one side for 30 minutes or longer. If you are stuck for time, then proceed immediately, but marinating the chicken even for 30 minutes will give the curry more depth of flavour.

2. For the curry itself, heat the oil in a deep wide pan and when hot, add the whole spices (cardamom, cloves, bay leaves, cinnamon, cumin and fennel seeds). Move them around the pan for 20 seconds before adding the diced onion and salt.

3. Keep the heat on a medium-low temperature and allow the onions to bronze. This will take around 8-10 minutes.

4. Meanwhile, grind the white poppy seeds in a pestle and mortar or spice grinder, adding a little water to loosen the powder into a thick paste. I tend to use a spice grinder to initially grind the poppy seeds and then transfer to my pestle and mortar for adding the water so that I can adjust the amount accordingly.

5. Add the poppy seed paste to the spiced onion, followed by the marinated chicken. Fold this into the gravy, then stir in the remaining water, fresh green chillies and sugar.

6. Cover the pan with a lid and simmer for 20 minutes, stirring intermittently. Taste the gravy, adding a little more salt or sugar as necessary. Continue to cook for a further 10 minutes, adding more water if it seems dry, then serve with a scattering of fresh coriander.

BREADS AND RICE

The main accompaniment to any curry is rice or bread. In India, people typically eat with their fingers which is a much more intuitive way of eating. I am always impressed by the elegance with which dishes are consumed, involving the precise mixing of rice or pinching with pieces of bread. Given that so many dishes involve delicious sauces and gravies, mopping up is key. While rice offers more uniformity, the differentiation coming only from the quality and grain, breads open up a wonderful array of possibilities that reflect regional cuisines. We can criss-cross India with bread: dosas and appam from the south to parathas and chapatis in the north. Importantly, making bread is a rewarding experience and something that cooks of all ages can get involved with.

Lemon Rice

Preparation time: 5 minutes
Cooking time: 20 minutes
Serves 4-6

This delicately spiced lemon rice is a wonderful way to bring colour, a hint of lemon and aromatic spices to an otherwise plain rice dish. It's easy and quick to make and hugely versatile.

1 tsp urid dal (optional)

1 tsp chana dal (optional)

1 handful of basmati rice (approx. 60g) per person

2 tbsp vegetable oil

2 tbsp peanuts and/or cashew nuts

1 tsp black or brown mustard seeds

10-15 curry leaves

¼ tsp asafoetida powder

2 small dried red chillies

1 tsp finely grated fresh ginger or ginger paste

½ tsp ground turmeric

1 lemon, zested

Salt, to taste

1. If using, soak the urid and chana dals in boiling water for 15 minutes. Meanwhile, wash the rice in cold water, drain and transfer it to a saucepan. Cover with fresh cold water so that when your index finger is resting on the top of the rice, the water comes up to the first crease in your index finger.

2. Gently bring the rice to the boil, then turn the heat down low and cover with a lid, ideally with a hole in to release the steam.

3. Cook on a low heat for 10 minutes, by which time small holes will begin to appear in the surface of the rice.

4. Do not lift the lid off the pan. Instead, remove it from the heat and allow the rice to steam for a further 5 minutes.

5. Heat the oil in a separate wide pan. When hot, add the soaked and drained dals, followed by the nuts. Move them around the pan so they don't burn.

6. Next, add the mustard seeds. They will begin to pop so take care. Stir in the curry leaves, asafoetida, dried red chillies and ginger. Finally, add the ground turmeric and mix in well.

7. Fold the cooked rice into the spice mixture along with the lemon zest and salt. Juice half of the zested lemon and stir this into the rice, adding more to taste if you wish, and serve hot.

Luchi

Preparation time: 15 minutes
Cooking time: 15 minutes
Makes 12

250g plain flour

½ tsp salt

1 tbsp vegetable or sunflower or rapeseed oil, plus extra for frying

150ml warm water

This dainty fried Bengali bread is addictively good and works so well with my coconut and sultana chana dal and spicy potato curry (see pages 66 and 106). It's very similar to the North Indian puri, the main difference being the flour used and the bronzing. Luchi use plain flour and remain white in colour, whereas puri are made with wholewheat flour and become bronzed.

1. Place the flour and salt in a bowl and add the tablespoon of oil. Using one hand, mix the flour and oil together and add the warm water a little at a time so that a dough begins to form. It is important to do this gradually in order to create a smooth and soft dough that's not too sticky or dry. If it remains sticky, add a dusting of extra flour.

2. Gently knead the dough for a couple of minutes so that it becomes nicely soft. Take a large plum-sized piece of dough and form a ball in your hand. Roll this out to approximately 10-12cm (4-5 inches) in diameter and 0.25cm thick. I find that it's a good idea to roll out all the discs first as the whole cooking process will be very quick.

3. Fill a medium-size deep pan halfway up with oil. Wait for the oil to reach a high temperature. To check whether it's at the optimum heat, simply pop a little bit of dough into the oil. If it fizzles and rises to the top, it's ready. If the oil is already bubbling it's too hot, so turn the heat down.

4. Place one of the discs into the oil and gently nudge the luchi with a spatula so it cooks evenly. It will immediately begin to puff up. After 5 seconds, turn it over and fry for a further 5-10 seconds before transferring the luchi to a plate lined with some kitchen roll. It will remain white or a very light bronze colour. If it turns bronze immediately and doesn't puff up, the heat is probably too high so turn it down before you fry another one.

5. Repeat the cooking process with the remaining discs of dough. Luchi are delicious eaten alongside many of the dals and vegetable curries in this book.

Naan Bread

These soft pillowy flatbreads, known as naan, are perfect for mopping up curries and dals but also work really well alongside barbecued meats or fish and salads. You don't need a tandoor oven; a frying pan, cast iron skillet or tawa will work just fine. To give your naan breads a Levantine twist, make them smaller and rounder, like a side plate, and gently brush olive oil and za'atar over them after cooking. They are great for breakfast too, especially dipped in eggs.

**Preparation time: 20 minutes +
1 hour resting
Cooking time: 20 minutes
Makes 10 medium naan**

1 tsp dried easy-bake yeast

1 tsp sugar

1 tbsp warm water

400g plain flour

2 tbsp vegetable oil

1 tsp salt

1 tsp baking powder

1 egg, beaten

100g full-fat plain yoghurt

100ml warm milk (full-fat or semi-skimmed)

1 tbsp melted ghee or olive oil

Toppings (optional)

1 tbsp nigella seeds

1 tbsp sesame seeds

1 tbsp chopped fresh coriander

2 cloves of garlic, finely chopped

For peshwari naan

2 tbsp desiccated coconut

1 tbsp flaked almonds

1 tbsp sultanas

1 tbsp water

1 tsp melted butter

1. Put the dried easy-bake yeast, sugar and warm water into a small bowl and allow the yeast to react with the sugar and froth up. Give the mixture a stir and then set aside for 15 minutes.

2. Put the flour into a large mixing bowl, make a well in the centre and pour in the oil, salt, baking powder, beaten egg and frothy yeast mixture.

3. Mix gently using your hands or a spoon and once it has become crumbly, add the yoghurt and continue to mix. Gradually add the warm milk until the mixture comes together. You may need slightly less than the full 100ml.

4. Dust a cold surface with a little plain flour and knead the dough on it for 5-7 minutes until it becomes soft and pliable, then return it to the bowl and gently smooth a little oil over the dough. Cover with cling film and leave in a warm room or oven (switched off but with the pilot light on) for 1 hour.

5. When the dough has rested and increased in size, split into about 10 evenly sized balls and begin to roll them out thinly, either into oval shapes or small round discs. Sprinkle each with a little extra flour to prevent the dough sticking to the surface. Pierce gently with a fork.

6. Heat a non-stick frying pan or tawa. When hot, place the first naan in the pan and leave for around 15-20 seconds before turning over and cooking for a further 15-20 seconds. Turn once more for a few seconds, or longer if it is not bronzing sufficiently. You need to make sure that your pan is sufficiently hot before starting to cook the naan.

7. Remove the naan from the pan and brush with a little of the melted ghee. Depending on your choice of toppings, sprinkle the naan with nigella or sesame seeds or fresh coriander. If you are making garlic naan, heat the chopped garlic in the ghee until it begins to bronze and then brush this on top of the naan.

8. Keep the cooked naan wrapped in a warm tea towel or in a warm oven (switched off with the door slightly open) while you finish the rest.

For peshwari naan

Blitz the ingredients together to form a rough paste. In Step 5, put a spoonful of this paste in the middle of a partially flattened dough ball, then bring the corners up and over the paste to form a pouch. Squeeze the ends to seal the pouch, then turn it over and gently flatten with your hand. Roll out gently and then proceed from Step 6. If you like, scatter some extra sultanas and flaked almonds on top to serve.

Chapati

Preparation time: 10 minutes + 30 minutes resting
Cooking time: 25 minutes
Makes 8

250g chapati/atta flour

1 tsp salt

2 tbsp vegetable or sunflower or rapeseed oil

190-200ml warm or hot, but not boiling, water

Ghee or oil, for brushing (optional)

Chapati, also known as roti and phulka, is unleavened flatbread and requires few ingredients. In most Indian households it's eaten hot and fresh off the pan, brushed with a little butter or ghee. Chapati flour, also known as atta, is finely milled wholewheat. To make an authentic chapati you do need chapati flour, as it has a high gluten content which allows it to be rolled thinly. It's easy to source from your local Asian grocer, some larger supermarkets or online. If you need to substitute this, you can opt for a 50/50 mix of wholemeal and plain flour.

1. Place the flour and salt in a bowl, then add the oil. Using one hand or a wooden spoon, mix the flour and oil together and add the water a little at a time. It's important to do this gradually in order to create a smooth and soft dough that's not too sticky or dry.

2. Gently knead the dough for around 5 minutes, or until it is nicely soft. Add a little more water or flour if needed. Once the dough is soft and no longer sticks to your fingers, put a little oil in the palm of your hands and wipe this over the dough. Cover with a damp cloth or cling film and leave to rest for a minimum of 30 minutes.

3. After this time, knead the dough for a couple of minutes and then break off a golf ball-sized piece. Dust it with flour and place on your clean work surface.

4. Use the palm of your hand to press down on the dough ball, creating a round disc. Gently roll it out evenly to the size of a side plate, approximately 18-20cm (7-8 inches) in diameter.

5. Heat a tawa, skillet or frying pan. When hot, reduce the heat to medium-low. Gently lift the chapati off your work surface and move it from one hand to the other to get rid of any excess flour, then place in the pan. Leave for around 20-30 seconds or until the underside starts to change colour. You will also notice small bubbles appearing on the dough. Flip it over and leave for another 30 seconds until brown spots begin to appear, checking intermittently that it is not burning. Turn over twice more to finish on both sides.

6. If you have a gas hob, remove the chapati from the pan and place directly onto the flame, using tongs. It will immediately begin to puff up. Once it does this, remove from the flame and set aside. Alternatively, leave the chapati on your skillet, press down gently with a spatula or tea towel on the edges and it will begin to puff up.

7. Brush the chapati with a little ghee or oil and either eat immediately or cover with tin foil or a clean tea towel to keep warm while you shape and cook the rest of the dough.

Plain Paratha

Preparation time: 30 minutes
Cooking time: 30 minutes
Makes 10

400g chapati/atta flour, plus extra for dusting

1 tsp salt

2 tbsp vegetable or rapeseed oil

190-200ml cold water

Melted butter or ghee, for brushing

Notes:

Substitutions: You can substitute ghee and butter with oil, but the overall taste and texture will not be as buttery and flaky. If you do not have chapati or wholemeal flour, opt for a mix of plain and white bread flour. It will still taste good but will not be as authentic.

Freezing: You can freeze paratha, but there are a few important steps. Fully cooked paratha do not freeze well. Instead, you can partially cook them on one side for 10-15 seconds and place on wax paper, then place in a sealable bag when cooled and freeze. You can also freeze raw paratha, first on a tray with wax paper between each one until they are stiff, then in a sealed bag. They will last for a couple of months this way, provided the bags are properly airtight. Cook the paratha from frozen and brush with ghee or oil while you are cooking them as usual.

Paratha are soft unleavened flatbreads like a chapati or roti, but they have multiple layers of dough which add a touch of flakiness. They are best made with chapati flour for the right texture. Plain flour won't give you as good results, so it is worth sourcing chapati flour. If you find this tricky, wholemeal flour is the best substitute. There are so many folding techniques for paratha, but I think the first one below is the easiest if you haven't made them before. I have also suggested an alternative, just in case you fancy a challenge!

1. Put the flour, salt and oil into a large bowl. Mix with your hand or a wooden spoon and then gradually add the cold water to make a soft ball of dough. You may need to add a little more water so adjust the amount accordingly.

2. Knead the dough for 1 minute until soft and pliable. Cover with a damp tea towel to stop it drying out and leave it to rest for 10 minutes to improve the texture.

3. Once rested, take a golf ball-sized amount of the dough and re-cover the remaining dough with the damp tea towel.

4. Put some flour on a side plate and press the dough ball into the flour on both sides. On a clean work surface, roll the dough into a circular disc approximately 18cm (7 inches) in diameter.

5. Brush a little melted butter or ghee over the dough and then fold the disc in half so you have a half moon shape. Brush on a little more butter or ghee, then fold once again so that you have a triangle of dough.

6. Dust the surface with flour and then roll out the dough triangle to over twice its original size, about 18-23cm (7-9 inches) at its widest part.

7. Another way to fold the paratha is to roll the dough into a square or rectangle, brush with a little ghee or butter and then fold both sides into the centre. Brush again lightly with ghee or butter and then fold in both ends so that you end up with a small square. Roll this square out to a larger square or rectangle. I suggest folding the paratha this way for the Kathi Rolls on page 58.

8. Heat up a frying pan or tawa over a medium-low heat. When the pan is hot, add the paratha. After 1 minute, flip it over and brush with ghee. Leave for a minute, then flip again and brush with a little more ghee while it cooks for a further minute.

9. Check whether the paratha is bronzing nicely and flip once again on both sides. Turn off the heat, then transfer the paratha to a piece of tin foil and cover to keep warm while you make the rest. Repeat the process above from Step 3 each time you make a paratha.

10. You can cook these ahead of time and reheat them wrapped in foil in the oven for 10 minutes at 180°C/160°C Fan/350°F/Gas Mark 4, although my preference is to eat them as soon as they are cooked.

Beetroot Paratha

Preparation time: 45 minutes
Cooking time: 30 minutes
Makes 10

1 large beetroot, peeled and finely grated

1 tsp finely grated fresh ginger or ginger paste

1 tsp finely grated garlic or garlic paste

1-2 small fresh green chillies, finely chopped

400g chapati/atta flour or wholemeal flour

1-2 tsp salt, to taste

1 tsp cumin seeds or ajwain/carom seeds

½ tsp amchoor/mango powder (optional)

½ tsp ground cumin

2 tbsp vegetable or rapeseed oil

190-200ml cold water

Extra flour, for dusting

Melted butter and ghee, for brushing

Once you have a handle on plain paratha, you can start getting inventive and making all kinds of wonderful combinations when it comes to adding flavours. One of my favourites is beetroot, which adds a vibrant colour and works so well with the cumin or ajwain seeds and the amchoor (mango) powder. Often parathas are stuffed with the filling, but for ease, I incorporate the beetroot and spices within the dough itself. You will see below that when it comes to folding the paratha, ghee (or melted butter) is used, which adds a touch of decadence.

1. Peel and finely grate the beetroot, do the same with the fresh ginger and garlic unless you are using paste, then finely chop the chillies and deseed them if you prefer less heat.

2. Put the flour, salt, cumin or ajwain seeds, amchoor powder and ground cumin into a large bowl and mix well.

3. Add the beetroot, ginger, garlic and chillies to the bowl along with the oil. Using your hand or a wooden spoon, mix all the ingredients together and then slowly add some of the cold water. Keep adding water until it all comes together, using more than the amount specified if required.

4. Knead the dough for a minute, then cover it with a damp cloth and leave for 10 minutes to improve the texture.

5. Once rested, tear off a golf ball-sized amount of dough and sprinkle with a little flour so it doesn't stick to your clean surface.

6. Roll it out into a circle approximately 18cm (7 inches) in diameter. Drizzle over and rub in a little melted butter or ghee on the surface of the paratha. Fold the circle in half so that you have a half moon shape, brush on a little more melted butter or ghee and fold again so that you now have a triangle.

7. Dust the dough or surface with flour as required to prevent sticking and then roll out the triangle to over twice its original size, about 18-23cm (7-9 inches) at its widest part.

8. Heat up a frying pan or tawa. When it is hot, reduce the heat to medium-low and add the paratha. After 1 minute, flip it over and brush with ghee (or oil). Leave for a minute and then flip again, brush with a little more ghee and cook for a further minute. Check to see it is bronzing nicely and then flip once again on both sides.

9. Turn off the heat and transfer the cooked paratha to a sheet of tin foil. Wrap it up to keep warm while you repeat the steps above to make and cook the rest of the paratha.

10. You can cook these ahead of time and then reheat them wrapped in foil in the oven for 10 minutes at 180°C/160°C Fan/350°F/Gas Mark 4, although I prefer to eat them as soon as they are cooked.

Notes: It's important to read the notes in the plain paratha recipe on page 180 which apply to this beetroot paratha too.

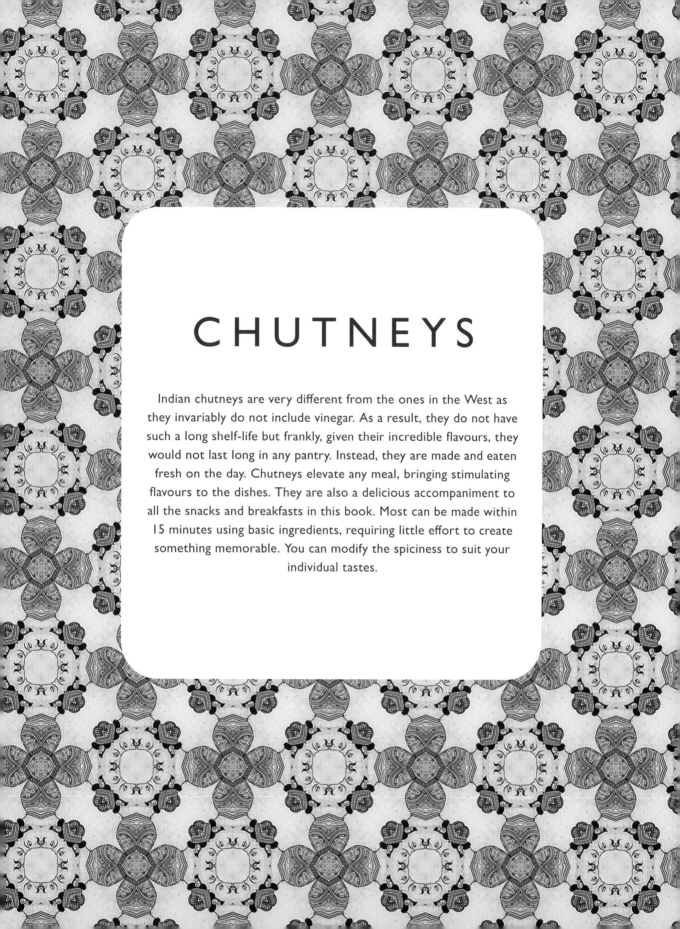

CHUTNEYS

Indian chutneys are very different from the ones in the West as they invariably do not include vinegar. As a result, they do not have such a long shelf-life but frankly, given their incredible flavours, they would not last long in any pantry. Instead, they are made and eaten fresh on the day. Chutneys elevate any meal, bringing stimulating flavours to the dishes. They are also a delicious accompaniment to all the snacks and breakfasts in this book. Most can be made within 15 minutes using basic ingredients, requiring little effort to create something memorable. You can modify the spiciness to suit your individual tastes.

Amma's Mango Chutney

Preparation time: 5 minutes
Cooking time: 8 minutes
Serves 4-6

2-3 small unripe green mangoes (or 1 large green mango)

1 tsp mustard or vegetable oil

2 small dried red chillies

1 tsp panch phoron/Bengali five spice

1 tsp finely grated fresh ginger

½-1 tsp salt, to taste

¼ tsp ground turmeric

110ml cold water

2 tsp cornflour

2-3 tbsp caster sugar

Notes: This chutney will keep in the fridge for a few days.

A beautiful mango tree stands outside the kitchen window of my mother-in-law's family home in Kolkata. These precious fruits are much prized, with the Alfonso mango often thought of as queen of all the mangoes. My chutney, however, does not require the sweet yellow juicy mangoes, instead the unripe small green variety. They can be found at any Indian grocer, but if you do not live near one, a regular large green mango from your local supermarket will still work. Just add less sugar, as it will be naturally sweeter than the unripe green mangoes which are sour.

1. Peel and destone the mangoes, then dice the flesh. If you are using unripe mangoes, boil them in a pan with some water and a pinch of salt for a couple of minutes to remove the acidity, as they can be very sour. Drain and set aside.

2. In a small pan, heat the oil and fry the dried red chillies so that they begin to darken. This will take around 1 minute. They may make you cough so pop on your extraction fan! Add the panch phoron, ginger, salt and ground turmeric to the pan along with the diced mango and 75ml of the cold water.

3. In a separate bowl, combine the cornflour with 35ml of cold water to create a smooth liquid. Immediately add this to the pan and stir it in. At this stage, add the sugar gradually so that you can check on the sweetness. If the mango is not too sour you may need a lot less sugar so do taste test as you go along.

4. Boil the chutney gently for 5-6 minutes. If you prefer a runnier chutney, add a little more water, or boil it for longer to thicken. Check the mango has softened before removing the pan from the heat.

5. Leave the chutney to cool and serve at room temperature or chilled.

Pomegranate Raita

Preparation time: 10 minutes
Serves 4-6

500g natural or Greek yoghurt

½ small cucumber, peeled and finely grated or chopped

½ small red onion, finely chopped

1 fresh green chilli, finely chopped

1 tbsp each finely chopped fresh mint and coriander

1 tsp each chaat masala powder and ground cumin

1 tsp salt, or to taste

2 tbsp pomegranate seeds

Raita is a refreshing yoghurt or curd condiment, which is great at cooling the palate when you are eating spicy food. The pomegranate seeds add pops of colour and sweetness. If you don't have any to hand though, you could always replace them with diced tomatoes.

1. Whisk the yoghurt in a bowl until smooth and then add all the other ingredients, holding back one tablespoon of the pomegranate seeds.

2. Taste to check the salt and spice levels.

3. To serve, scatter the raita with the remaining pomegranate seeds.

Coconut Chutney

Preparation time: 15 minutes +
30 minutes freezing if using my
coconut hack
Cooking time: 5 minutes
Serves 4-6

1 heaped tbsp chana dal or blanched
peanuts

100g fresh coconut, roughly chopped
or grated

2.5cm (1 inch) fresh ginger

1 fresh green chilli

1 tsp lemon juice

½ tsp salt

For the tempering

1 tsp coconut or rapeseed or vegetable
oil

Small pinch of asafoetida powder

½ tsp each black or brown mustard
seeds and cumin seeds

1 small dried red chilli

5 fresh curry leaves

Coconut chutney is a staple of South Indian cuisine where coconut palms are in abundance. It's typically served at breakfast with idlis, dosa, upma, uttapam and appam/hoppers. It is also the perfect accompaniment to many curries, making any meal feel that extra bit special.

1. If you are using a whole fresh coconut, place it in your freezer for around 30 minutes. Remove and use a rolling pin to bash the outer husk of the coconut. You will find that having put the coconut in the freezer for that short amount of time will make it easier to open. It should crack more easily and allow you to get to the white flesh of the coconut.

2. In a frying pan, dry roast the chana dal or blanched peanuts so that they begin to bronze. Transfer them to a blender along with the coconut, ginger, green chilli, lemon juice and salt. Add a little water to loosen the mixture and blitz, then add a little more water if you require a smoother consistency. The chutney shouldn't be too thick or too runny: the consistency of double cream should be about right.

3. For the tempering, heat the oil in a frying pan and add the remaining ingredients. They will begin to sizzle and possibly spit so be careful. Move around the pan for 30 seconds and then pour directly over the chutney. Stir in gently before serving.

South Indian Tomato and Date Chutney

Preparation time: 10 minutes
Cooking time: 10 minutes
Serves 4-6

2½ tbsp vegetable oil

1 tbsp chana dal

2 small dried red chillies

½ large white onion, roughly chopped

1 heaped tsp each grated or chopped
fresh ginger and garlic

3 large tomatoes, roughly chopped

2 dried dates, roughly chopped

1 tsp salt

For the tempering

½ tsp black or brown mustard seeds

¼ tsp asafoetida powder

6 curry leaves

The taste and texture of this chutney is very different from my Bengali tomato chutney. This one is smooth and found in South India, often at breakfast alongside dosa, idly, appam or medu vada. It will last a few days in the fridge, but this quantity is normally finished in one sitting.

1. Heat a tablespoon of the oil in a frying pan and then add the uncooked chana dal. Move it around the pan until it browns in colour. This will take around 20-30 seconds so do not take your eyes off it. Transfer to a small bowl to cool.

2. Blitz the cooled chana dal in a spice grinder or grind in a pestle and mortar. It does not have to be a powder but should be broken up.

3. Using the same pan, add a little more oil if required and fry the dried red chillies. Move them around the pan so they begin to darken, then add the onion.

4. Keep the heat low and allow the onion to soften over the next 4 minutes without bronzing. Add the ginger, garlic, tomatoes, dates and salt. Move everything around the pan for 3 minutes.

5. Return the blitzed chana dal to the pan and stir well. Remove from the heat, then blitz the contents to form a smooth chutney. Place in a serving bowl.

6. For the tempering, heat the remaining oil in a small clean pan and then add the mustard seeds, asafoetida and curry leaves. Move them around the pan for a minute and then pour directly on top of the chutney. Stir in just before serving.

Carrot Chutney

Preparation time: 10 minutes
Cooking time: 12 minutes
Serves 4-6

2 tbsp coconut or vegetable oil

1 tsp urid dal

2 tsp chana dal

2 dried red chillies

1 small onion, finely chopped

2 cloves of garlic, roughly chopped

½ tsp finely chopped or grated fresh ginger

1 tsp salt, or to taste

½ tsp concentrated tamarind paste or a small (2p size) piece of stoneless tamarind (optional)

4 large carrots, cubed or grated

1 tbsp fresh grated or desiccated coconut

1 tsp brown or black mustard seeds

8 curry leaves

I became hooked on this South Indian chutney when I was in Kerala, often starting the day with some alongside my breakfast dosa. It's sweet and hot, with some pleasing tangy sour notes if you add tamarind. The urid and chana lentils don't need soaking as they cook in the hot oil, which also adds another layer of flavour to the chutney.

1. Heat half of the oil in a pan and when hot, add the dal and chillies. Allow them to darken slightly over the next minute.

2. Add the onion, garlic, ginger and salt to the pan and stir everything together. Allow the onions to soften and stop smelling raw over the next 3-4 minutes, without bronzing.

3. Add the tamarind and carrots, then after a minute add 4 tablespoons of water to help the carrots soften slightly. Stir intermittently over the next 3-4 minutes.

4. Transfer the mixture to a mini blender and add the coconut. Blend briefly, then add up to 30ml of water to loosen as required. Once the chutney is smooth and not too thick, transfer it to a small bowl. Taste test and add more salt if necessary.

5. Finish by tempering the spices. Heat the remaining oil in the original pan and when hot, add the mustard seeds and curry leaves. Move around the pan for 20 seconds and then pour directly on top of the chutney. Stir gently and the chutney is ready.

6. Serve at room temperature. It will keep in the fridge for up to 5 days in a sealed container, although it will normally be finished in a couple of sittings!

Notes: Carrot chutney is pictured on page 47.

Bengali Tomato Chutney

Preparation time: 10 minutes
Cooking time: 6-8 minutes
Serves 4-6

1 tbsp rapeseed or vegetable oil

2 small dried red chillies

1 tsp black or brown mustard seeds

2.5cm (1 inch) fresh ginger, grated or finely chopped

300g fresh tomatoes, halved or quartered

¼ tsp salt

4 tsp caster sugar, or to taste

3 pieces of dried mango, roughly chopped (optional, or use 3 dried apricots, prunes or dates)

This is a very typical Bengali tomato chutney, or achaar as it is known in India. The sweet notes from the added fruit and sugar balance out the savoury chilli, mustard seeds, salt and ginger really well. It's not meant to be super smooth like my other tomato chutney.

1. Warm the oil in a pan on a medium heat and fry the dried red chillies until they begin to turn black. This will take a few minutes and may make you cough, so pop your extraction fan on!

2. Add the mustard seeds, fresh ginger, chopped tomatoes, salt, sugar and dried fruit if using. As they warm up, squash the tomatoes with the back of a fork or spoon so they release their juices and no longer hold their shape.

3. After 3-4 minutes, taste the chutney and add more salt or sugar as required. Leave it to simmer for a few more minutes or until the tomatoes have completely softened.

4. Transfer the chutney into a small serving bowl to cool, then serve at room temperature. It will last in the fridge for a few days.

Notes: Bengali tomato chutney is pictured on page 31.

Spicy Caramelised Onion Sambol

Preparation time: 10 minutes
Cooking time: 25 minutes
Serves 4-6

5 large red onions

2 tbsp vegetable or rapeseed oil

3 cloves, lightly bruised

4 green cardamom pods, bruised

7.5cm (3 inch) pandan leaf, halved lengthways

10-15 curry leaves

1-2 fresh green chillies, sliced horizontally

3 cloves of garlic, thinly sliced

1 tsp each ground turmeric, chilli flakes and chilli powder

1 tbsp Maldive fish chips, crushed into a coarse powder (optional)

¾ tsp salt, or to taste

2 tbsp light brown sugar or jaggery

This deliciously spiced Sri Lankan onion sambol, known as seeni sambol, is always a hit. It involves a lot of stirring, but the effort is worth it. Unlike the British version of onion chutney, which often requires vinegar, this one does not and therefore should be consumed within a week.

1. First, thinly slice the red onions into half-moons using a mandoline or the thin slicer mode on a Magimix food processor.

2. Heat the oil in a large deep pan, then add the lightly bruised cloves, green cardamom, pandan leaf, curry leaves, green chillies and sliced garlic. Move everything around the pan for a minute to release the aromas before adding the red onion.

3. After about 10 minutes, the onions will become more translucent in colour and over the 10 minutes after that, they will become bronzed and will have shrunk to half their size. You need to keep stirring the onions every 30 seconds or so throughout this process, and keep the heat on medium-low. Don't rush this stage as the onions need to caramelise properly.

4. Add the ground turmeric, chilli flakes, chilli powder, crushed Maldive fish chips (if using) and salt. Stir everything into the onions and continue to cook while stirring on a low heat.

5. After a few more minutes, add the sugar and stir once again for another 3-4 minutes. The onions will now be a dark brown colour and will have the right balance of sweet, salty and spicy flavours.

Notes: Spicy caramelised onion sambol is pictured on page 35.

Tamarind and Date Chutney

Preparation time: 10 minutes
Serves 4-6

120g dates

150ml water

½ tsp Kashmiri chilli powder

½ lemon, juiced

½ tsp salt, or to taste

1 tsp caster sugar

2 tsp tamarind concentrate paste

The tart tangy taste of tamarind (try saying that fast!) works so well with the sweetness of dates, making this chutney the perfect accompaniment to pretty much any Indian snack or even cheese. It's quick and easy to make, requires no cooking whatsoever and will last in the fridge for up to a week.

1. Before putting the dates into your blender, chop them up and remove the stones. Add a little of the water to help soften them and blitz to a rough paste.

2. Add the Kashmiri chilli powder, lemon juice, salt, sugar and 1 teaspoon of the tamarind paste to the blender, then blitz once again. Add enough water so that it becomes smooth.

3. Taste test the chutney and then add the remaining teaspoon of tamarind paste. Add more water as required so that your chutney is the same consistency as tomato ketchup. You may find you don't need to use all the water, depending on what dates you use.

4. Taste test again to check the balance of salty, sweet, tangy and sour flavours and add more sugar or salt as required.

Coriander, Mint and Lime Chutney

Preparation time: 10 minutes
Serves 4-6

20g unsalted cashews or blanched peanuts

2 handfuls of fresh coriander leaves

1 handful of fresh mint leaves

1 heaped tsp finely grated fresh ginger

1 fresh green chilli, deseeded for less heat (optional)

1 lime, juiced

2 tsp caster sugar, or to taste

½ tsp salt, or to taste

25ml water

This deliciously zingy and versatile chutney is a great accompaniment for many Indian snacks, including samosas, daler bora and Indian savoury doughnuts. The key is to create the right balance of sweet, salty, hot and sour flavours. It will keep in a sealed container in the fridge for up to a week.

1. Begin by soaking the cashews or peanuts in warm water for 5 minutes to soften them. Drain and transfer to a blender.

2. Add the fresh herbs, ginger, chilli if using, lime juice, sugar and salt to the nuts and blitz, adding enough of the water to loosen it slightly. You are aiming for a smooth chutney which has the consistency of a dipping sauce.

3. If you had a juicy lime, you probably won't need to add much more water, but if the chutney remains too thick, add a little extra water to loosen it. Add more salt, sugar, chilli or lime juice to suit your individual taste.

Notes: You can also stir this chutney into Greek yoghurt if you fancy giving it a creamier spin.

SWEET TREATS AND DRINKS

I'll be honest with you. I do not have a sweet tooth, preferring a light touch of sweetness at the end of a meal as opposed to a massive sugar rush. This section does have some authentic sweet delights, but also some of my European desserts that have been given a touch of spice or freshness. I wanted to include recipes that you will want to cook and that will pair well with the other savoury recipes in this book. I cook all of these through the changing seasons; some offer refreshment on hot summer days, such as my tamarind sharbat, which will perhaps be a new taste sensation for some of you. My chocolate, chilli and cinnamon fondants will offer comfort on cold wintery nights and a mug of my masala chai will lift the spirits whatever the season. Like a good dessert, this chapter is short but sweet, and I hope the recipes I have included will become firm favourites in your own kitchen.

Chilli and Mint Choc Chip Ice Cream

**Preparation time: 30 minutes +
overnight**
Cooking time: 30 minutes
Makes 1 tub (9 x 5 x 8cm)

600ml full-fat milk

600ml double cream

1 vanilla pod, split open lengthways

80g fresh mint leaves, stalks trimmed

1-2 fresh green chillies, split open
lengthways

8 medium egg yolks

200g caster sugar

1-2 tsp green food colouring (optional)

70g dark chocolate drops or broken up
chocolate

Growing up, mint choc chip was one of my absolute favourite ice cream flavours.
As my blog is called Chilli and Mint it felt only natural to include this recipe in my
book, even though it is not strictly 'Indian' in origin. This is ice cream made the
Western way, which as you can see contains eggs, giving the ice cream a custard
base. This is unlike kulfi, the Indian version of ice cream, which takes less time and
contains no milk or eggs (see my recipe on page 208).

1. If you are going to use an ice cream maker, place the bowl part in the freezer
    the night before you plan to make the ice cream.

2. The next day, gently heat the milk and double cream in a heavy-based pan.
    Scrape the seeds from the vanilla pod and place both the pod and seeds into
    the pan.

3. Add the fresh mint leaves and green chilli, including the seeds, to the pan. Use
    a spatula to stir the mixture intermittently as it simmers gently for 5 minutes.

4. Remove the pan from the heat and allow the mint, chilli and vanilla to infuse
    the milk and cream for 1 hour. Strain the contents of the pan and discard the
    mint, vanilla pod and chilli.

5. In a clean bowl, combine the egg yolks and caster sugar with an electric whisk
    until smooth.

6. Gently reheat the infused milk and cream in the pan, then pour the hot liquid
    slowly and gradually into the egg and sugar mixture. Whisk continually until it
    has all combined.

7. Return the mixture to the heavy-based pan and keep the heat low. Do not
    let it boil, or else your eggs may curdle. Allow the temperature to gently rise
    and the custard to thicken until it coats the back of your spatula. This will take
    around 8-10 minutes.

8. Remove the pan from the heat and immediately place it in a sink of iced water
    so the pan is partly submerged. Allow to cool completely.

9. Once cooled, whisk in the green food colouring if using – this won't alter the
    flavour! – then stir through the chocolate.

10. Pour the mixture into your chilled bowl and churn with the ice cream maker.
    This usually takes around 20-30 minutes or until it has come together in a soft
    scoop consistency.

11. You can then eat the ice cream immediately or place it into a freezer-proof
    container to harden further. Cover with cling film, if it doesn't have a lid, to
    prevent frosting.

12. If you do not have an ice-cream maker, pour the ice cream into a freezer-
    proof container with a lid and place in the freezer for 45 minutes, then remove
    it and give the ice cream a good stir, removing any crystals that have formed
    at the side of the container. Return to the freezer and leave for another
    30 minutes, then stir again. Keep repeating this until frozen.

Notes: Keep the leftover egg whites from this recipe to make my tropical pavlova
(see page 210).

Masala Chai

Preparation time: 5 minutes
Cooking time: 10 minutes
Makes 6 small cups

600ml water

7.5cm (3 inches) fresh ginger

7 green cardamom pods

5 black peppercorns

3 cloves

½ tsp fennel seeds

¼ tsp ground cinnamon or 7.5cm (3 inches) cinnamon stick or bark

400ml milk of your choice

2-3 tsp loose black tea leaves

3 tsp sugar or jaggery

There is something incredibly comforting and nourishing about a cup of masala chai, no matter what time of year it is. In the autumn and winter months in the UK, I love to return to the house after a bracing walk and make myself some warming spiced tea to sip beside the fire. It works equally well in the hot Indian sunshine; stopping at a chai wallah a couple of times a day is a ritual I greatly enjoy. That rush of sugar and spice in milky tea really lifts the spirit and brings me some inner zen.

1. First, bring the water to the boil. While it heats up, cut the fresh ginger into rounds, leaving the skin on, then use a pestle and mortar (or the end of a rolling pin) to open the green cardamom pods and bruise the black peppercorns and ginger to release more flavour.

2. Place all the spices in the boiling water and swirl them around the pan. Simmer gently for a couple of minutes.

3. Add the milk of your choice to the pan and gently bring the mixture back to the boil. In India, they typically use a full-fat milk.

4. Allow the chai to reach boiling point a couple of times so it becomes frothy, turning the heat down or off to prevent it from spilling over. It all happens quite fast so keep a close eye on the pan.

5. Now add the loose black tea leaves and stir well before adding the sugar or jaggery. If you prefer a sweeter chai, add a little more sugar.

6. Let the chai simmer for 5 minutes, turning the heat down or off each time it looks like it might boil over.

7. To serve, strain the hot liquid into small cups and enjoy your milky masala chai. The wallahs in India often pour the tea from an impressive height to add extra froth before serving it. I'll leave it up to you regarding how authentic you wish to be at this point!

Chaat Masala Fruit Salad

Preparation time: 15 minutes
Serves 4

2 mangoes

2 apples

6 strawberries

10 white or black grapes

1 banana

1 tbsp lemon or lime juice

1 heaped tsp chaat masala powder

½ tsp Kashmiri chilli powder (optional, add less if using a different chilli powder)

Pinch of sea salt or black salt

This fruit salad is deliciously zingy, tangy, salty and sweet. It works really well in the heat as a snack or palate cleanser at the end of a meal. Chaat masala is a wonderful spice mix combining black salt, black pepper, cumin, coriander, cloves, nutmeg, asafoetida, caraway, dried mango and mint. Feel free to add or swap some of the fruits here for melon, pomegranate or oranges.

1. First, prepare all the fruit. Peel the mangoes and core the apples, then cut both into bite-size pieces. Halve or quarter the strawberries, depending on their size, then halve the grapes and deseed if needed. Peel the banana, halve it lengthways and cut into thick slices.

2. Mix all the fruit, except the banana, together in a large bowl. Gently stir in the lemon or lime juice, chaat masala and Kashmiri chilli powders, and salt.

3. Add the banana and carefully give the salad a final mix before serving.

Tamarind Sharbat

Preparation time: 30 minutes
Cooking time: 5 minutes
Serves 6

100g tamarind pulp (from a block)

200ml boiling water

2 tbsp jaggery or granulated sugar

⅛ tsp (small pinch) black salt/kala namak

1 litre cold water (still or sparkling)

14 ice cubes

Fresh mint leaves, to garnish

1 lime, thinly sliced

Sweet and sour notes dance on your tongue with this cooling chilled summer drink, which is similar in essence to a Western cordial. You can find tamarind blocks at Asian grocers. If you can, opt for seedless tamarind blocks which will be easier to work with. They last for months in the fridge so you can also use them for some of my curries in this book.

1. First, place the tamarind in a bowl and cover it with the boiling water. Break up the tamarind with the back of a spoon as best you can, then leave it to soak for 15-20 minutes.

2. Break the soaked tamarind up again and pour the contents of the bowl into a sieve over a clean bowl. Push the tamarind through the sieve, scraping the bottom to extract all the paste. Once you've got as much as possible in the bowl, discard any solids left in the sieve.

3. Place the tamarind mixture into a jug blender. Add the jaggery or sugar and the black salt. Black salt has a very sulphurous aroma, like hard-boiled eggs, but it gives the sharbat a tangy taste. If you have not tried it before it may take you by surprise. Personally, I love it.

4. Next, add the cold water and ice cubes to the blender, then blitz for 10 seconds. Pour the mixture into a chilled jug with some more ice. Leave in the fridge until ready to drink.

5. Serve each glass with a couple of mint leaves and a thin slice of fresh lime on top. This is so refreshing to sip on hot summer days.

Notes: You can make this drink alcoholic if you like by adding a shot of gin or vodka to each glass before filling them up with the tamarind sharbat.

Chocolate, Chilli and Cinnamon Fondants

Preparation time: 15 minutes
Cooking time: 30 minutes
Serves 8

2 tbsp butter, melted

Cocoa powder, for dusting

200g cooking chocolate (I use 100g dark and 100g milk, but it's up to you)

200g unsalted butter

4 eggs

4 egg yolks

200g caster sugar

200g plain flour

½ -1 tsp chilli flakes, to taste (optional)

1 tsp ground cinnamon

2 tsp icing sugar

If you want to serve a highly original sweet treat that will elicit gasps and whoops of joy from your guests, then this is the one for you. If you follow my directions to the letter you can't go wrong. Famous last words, I know! I like to add a little chilli and cinnamon to give it an Indian twist and eat them fresh out the oven with cardamom Chantilly cream (see my pavlova recipe on page 210). Simply glorious.

1. Use the melted butter to brush the insides of 8 fondant moulds and then place them in the freezer for 10 minutes. Once chilled, coat the moulds again with melted butter, immediately followed by a little cocoa powder. Tap to remove the excess and make sure you completely cover the insides of the moulds.

2. Unless you are making these ahead of time and freezing the fondants, preheat your oven to 200°C/180°C Fan/400°F/Gas Mark 6.

3. Gently boil some water in a pan that you can sit a heatproof bowl over without it touching the water. Break up the cooking chocolate into the bowl, cube and add the butter, then let them melt gradually, stirring at intervals.

4. In a mixing bowl, whisk the eggs, egg yolks and sugar together until the mixture thickens slightly. This will take a couple of minutes. Add the flour and then gradually pour in the melted chocolate and butter. Continue to whisk until well combined.

5. Add the chilli flakes and ground cinnamon, then taste to check the flavour and add more chilli or cinnamon if you like.

6. Transfer the fondant mixture into a measuring jug so it's easier to pour, then fill each prepared mould three quarters full.

7. At this stage you have two options: either put them in the freezer for another time, or if you want to eat them immediately, cook them on the middle shelf of the preheated oven for 10 minutes, which makes them soft and gooey in the middle. If you want a firmer centre, leave them for 11-12 minutes, and if cooking from frozen they will need 15-17 minutes.

8. Once cooked, leave the fondants to rest for a minute before placing a plate on top of the first mould and turning so that it is the right way up. The mould will easily come away from the chocolate fondant. Should it need a helping hand, gently shake the mould while holding the plate firmly in place. Repeat to turn out all the fondants.

9. Dust with icing sugar and serve immediately with cardamom Chantilly cream (see my pavlova recipe on page 210).

Panna Cotta with Raspberry Coulis

**Preparation time: 15 minutes +
infusing and setting time
Cooking time: 15 minutes
Makes 6**

350ml milk

350ml double cream

90g caster sugar

3 cinnamon sticks

1 tsp ground nutmeg

6 fine leaf gelatine leaves

For the raspberry coulis

200g fresh or frozen raspberries

1 tbsp icing sugar

½ lemon, juiced

Panna cotta is a wonderfully light dessert not dissimilar to the Bengali delicacy, mishti doi. It marries well with Indian food and adds the perfect sweet touch at the end of a meal, complemented here by a slightly tangy raspberry coulis.

1. Combine the milk, cream, caster sugar, cinnamon and nutmeg in a saucepan. Gently bring to the boil so that the sugar dissolves and then immediately turn off the heat. Allow this mixture to rest for 1 hour so that the cinnamon and nutmeg infuses the milk and cream.

2. After resting, remove the cinnamon sticks and then reheat the mixture in the pan so that it warms up but does not boil.

3. Meanwhile, cover the gelatine leaves with cold water in a bowl and leave for 10 minutes to soften. Using your hands, squeeze the water out of the gelatine and add the softened leaves to the warm milk and cream mixture. Stir well until the gelatine dissolves.

4. Using some kitchen roll, lightly oil the sides of 6 dariole moulds or ramekins and then fill them with the panna cotta mixture. Leave to cool completely before placing them in the fridge to set. You can leave these overnight or for a couple of hours minimum.

5. For the raspberry coulis, place the fresh or frozen raspberries, icing sugar and lemon juice in a pan over a gentle heat to simmer for 5 minutes. Allow the raspberries to soften completely and the sugar to dissolve. Use a spatula to help break up the raspberries.

6. Blitz the mixture with a handheld blender and then strain through a sieve. Discard all the raspberry seeds and then pour the coulis into a small jug. Allow to cool and then cover and place in the fridge until ready to use.

7. When you are ready to serve, remove the panna cotta from the fridge and leave to stand at room temperature for 10 minutes. Use a knife to gently loosen the tops around the edge, then place a small plate over the mould or ramekin. Flip it over, give it a good shake and the panna cotta should be released. Try a couple of times this way, and if it really needs a helping hand, pour a small amount of warm water into a bowl and sit the dariole mould in it for a maximum of 5 seconds. Dry the bottom of the mould and then try turning out again.

8. Plate up the unmoulded panna cotta, pour a little raspberry coulis over each one and enjoy.

Sesame Seed and Pistachio Balls

Preparation time: 10-15 minutes
Cooking time: 10 minutes
Makes 34

250g white sesame seeds

2 tbsp ghee

2 tbsp water

250g jaggery or muscovado sugar

50g pistachios, roughly chopped

Known as tiler naru in Bengal, these sweet nutty treats are hard on the outside and chewy in the centre. They are made with white sesame seeds and jaggery, sometimes with the addition of pistachios, almonds or sunflower seeds. You can often find them in the pantries of Bengali kitchens and misti dokan (sweet shops) throughout the year, probably because they are too tasty to keep just for the Bengali religious festival season which falls around October. They are great to make ahead of time and store in a glass container for edible gifts, especially at Christmas.

1. Warm a large frying pan on a low heat and then add the white sesame seeds. Move them around the pan for a couple of minutes until the nutty aroma is released and they begin to lightly bronze but not fully brown. Remove them from the pan and pour into a bowl.

2. Next, grease a large plate with a little ghee or oil. This will stop the mixture from sticking to the plate later on.

3. Using the same large frying pan, heat the ghee and then add water and jaggery or sugar. Keep it on a low heat. At first the mixture will seem thick, but as it warms up it will become thinner and then begin to bubble and turn a darker brown.

4. To check the consistency is right, dip a spatula into the mixture then carefully touch it with your index finger and press the syrup against your thumb. As you move them apart, the syrup should create a string, which means it is ready. It only takes about 3-4 minutes.

5. Now you must work quickly: turn off the heat and stir the sesame seeds and pistachios into the syrup. Fold it well and then pour the mixture onto the greased plate.

6. Leave to cool for a minute and then put a little oil or ghee on the palms of your hands. Take a little of the mixture at a time and roll it into small balls.

7. Space the balls out on a clean plate and allow them to cool completely before storing in a glass container. They will last for a few months like this but are great as an after dinner treat or with a cup of masala chai, so may not be around that long!

Strawberry and Black Pepper Kulfi

Preparation time: 10 minutes + 3-4 hours freezing
Cooking time: 15 minutes
Makes 6 lollies or ramekins

200g fresh strawberries, halved

½ tbsp caster sugar

1 tsp freshly ground black pepper

200ml double cream

200ml condensed milk

Kulfi is India's answer to ice cream, which is both delicious and very simple in that it requires no churning and is ready to eat within a few hours. Its origins stem from the Mughal era when flavours such as pistachio, rose, cardamom, orange and saffron were infused into the creamy cooling kulfi, offering much respite during the hot summer days. The idea of strawberries and black pepper came from a memorable meal I ate in the early 2000s at the Painted Heron restaurant in Chelsea, which had strawberry and black pepper curry on the menu. A revelation.

1. Preheat your oven to 170°C/150°C Fan/325°F/Gas Mark 3 and place the halved strawberries on a baking tray. Sprinkle the caster sugar and half of the freshly ground black pepper over them, then place the tray in the oven for 10 minutes. This helps to accentuate the flavours.

2. Transfer the heated strawberries to a blender and blitz until you have a smooth purée. Pour this through a sieve and then transfer it back into the blender.

3. Add the double cream, condensed milk and remaining black pepper to the blender. Blitz this mixture until smooth, then taste and add a little more pepper to balance the sweetness if needed.

4. Divide the mixture between 6 silicone ice lolly moulds or ramekins and then leave them in the freezer for at least 4 hours, until the kulfi sets completely.

5. When you're ready to remove the kulfi from the moulds or ramekins, dip them in a shallow bowl filled with warm water for a few seconds and go round the edge with a knife to loosen it. Put a bowl or side plate over the top of the ramekin and then flip over to release the kulfi, or simply slide them out of the lolly moulds.

Notes: If you want to make a bigger batch, double or triple the ingredient quantities and freeze the kulfi in a Tupperware instead of individual moulds or ramekins.

Tropical Pavlova with Cardamom Cream

**Preparation time: 25 minutes +
cooling time
Cooking time: 1 hour 15 minutes
Serves 8**

For the meringue

4 egg whites

200g caster sugar

1 tsp cornflour

1 tsp vanilla essence

1 tsp white wine vinegar

For the Chantilly cream

300ml double cream

2 tbsp super fine caster sugar

7 green cardamom pods, seeds
extracted and ground (husks discarded)

For the topping

1 large mango, peeled, destoned and
cubed

2 kiwi, peeled and sliced

2 tbsp fresh pomegranate seeds

1 sprig of fresh mint, finely chopped

½ lime, juiced

This recipe takes a traditional British dessert and gives it an Indian makeover with cardamom-flavoured Chantilly cream and fresh mango, kiwi, pomegranate and mint. It makes a lovely alternative to the berry version and is very statuesque, as a pavlova should be. I tend to make one large pavlova, but you can make 4-6 smaller meringue nests if you want to have individual servings.

1. For the meringue, preheat the oven to 150°C/130°C Fan/300°F/Gas Mark 2. Whisk the egg whites together until they form stiff peaks, then add the caster sugar a tablespoon at a time and keep whisking gently.

2. Once the sugar is incorporated, fold in the cornflour, vanilla and white wine vinegar until well combined.

3. Draw around an upturned dinner plate on a large sheet of baking paper, then remove the plate and spread the meringue mixture out evenly within the circle you've drawn.

4. Place the meringue in the preheated oven and immediately turn the temperature down to 120°C/100°C Fan/250°F/Gas Mark ½. Bake for 1 hour 15 minutes and then turn off the oven completely and leave the oven door ajar as the meringue cools. Do not take it out of the oven until it is completely cool.

5. For the Chantilly cream, simply whip the double cream and then slowly add the caster sugar and ground cardamom seeds until it is light and fluffy. Store in the fridge until ready to use.

6. Now prepare the fresh fruit and mint. Just before serving the pavlova, gently spread the Chantilly cream over the top of the cooled meringue, being careful not to break it up.

7. Distribute the mango evenly over the cream followed by the kiwi, pomegranate seeds and mint. Finally, drizzle the lime juice over the fruit and serve the pavlova.

Notes: The lightly spiced thick cardamom cream can be made in advance, covered and stored in the fridge. It also goes well with my chocolate, chilli and cinnamon fondants on page 202.

SPICE BLENDS

Spices and history are interwoven: maritime adventures; trading outposts; fortunes made and lost; empires built; and no small part played by violence. The basis of Indian cuisine and its very DNA is spice. Thankfully, we now have everything available at supermarkets globally. The choice can seem overwhelming, but in these recipes, I guide you through the remarkable range of tastes and flavours that can be created in your kitchen. Knowing how to blend and grind spices is all part of the everyday alchemy of Indian cuisine. It is an inherent skill in India among home cooks but one I have unpicked, having initially approached it as a novice. Spice need not be overbearing and clumsy. It can be elegant, it can bring life, it can soothe, it can excite, it can calm, it can balance, and it can surprise.

Rasam Powder

Preparation time: 5 minutes
Cooking time: 5 minutes
Makes approx. 120g

6 tbsp coriander seeds

2 tbsp toor dal

2 tbsp black peppercorns

2 tbsp cumin seeds

I tsp fenugreek seeds

4-7 dried small red chillies

10-15 curry leaves

I tsp ground turmeric

¼ tsp asafoetida powder

Rasam powder is an integral part of the South Indian soup called rasam. The soup itself is hot, sour, sweet and salty and is one of my go-to lunches for a little pick-me-up, especially during the winter months when I need warming from the inside. You can make it as hot as you want depending on the variety of red chillies that you use. If you want less heat, opt for dried red Kashmiri chillies.

1. Heat a heavy-based pan over a medium heat and add the coriander seeds, toor dal, black peppercorns, cumin seeds and fenugreek seeds. Move them around the pan with a spatula or wooden spoon for 2 minutes until lightly bronzed and aromatic, then pour into a bowl.

2. Using the same pan, allow it to heat up once again and then add the dried chillies and curry leaves. Move them around the pan for a minute.

3. Add the ground turmeric and asafoetida powder to the pan and stir for 20 seconds, then pour the contents into the bowl of spices.

4. Put the contents of the bowl into a spice grinder and grind to a smooth powder. Store in a sealed glass container out of direct light, somewhere cool.

Notes: Dried red chillies range dramatically in heat levels. Dried Kashmiri chillies are less hot, so adding 7 will be fine. If you have a hot variety, 3-4 should be sufficient. Start by making this powder with fewer chillies until you are comfortable with the heat level of the chillies you buy.

Sambar Masala

Preparation time: 5 minutes
Cooking time: 7-10 minutes
Makes a small pot

I ½ tbsp chana dal

I ½ tbsp white urid dal

I tbsp toor dal

4 tbsp coriander seeds

I tbsp cumin seeds

I tsp black peppercorns

I tsp black mustard seeds

¾ tsp fenugreek seeds

8-10 dried Kashmiri chillies (or a hotter variety if preferred)

10-15 curry leaves

½ tsp ground turmeric

½ tsp asafoetida powder

Sambar masala is an integral component of the ubiquitous lentil soup eaten in South India and Sri Lanka, known as sambar. You can buy a store-bought powder but making your own is easy and so satisfying. It takes minutes to prepare, although you do need a spice grinder.

1. Put a frying pan over a low heat and when hot, add the chana, urid and toor dal. Move them around the pan for 3-4 minutes until bronzed, then pour into a bowl to cool.

2. Using the same pan, toast the coriander, cumin, peppercorns, black mustard seeds and fenugreek. Move them around the pan so they do not burn but their aromas are released. This will take I minute. Pour the spices into the same bowl as the dals.

3. Using the same pan once again, heat the chillies and curry leaves until the chillies darken. This will not take much longer than a couple of minutes.

4. Put the chillies and curry leaves into the bowl of spices, then add the ground turmeric and asafoetida.

5. Pour the mixture into a spice grinder and blend. You will probably have to do this in 2 or 3 batches depending on the size of your spice grinder. Transfer to a jar and seal to store.

Sri Lankan Roasted Curry Powder

Preparation time: 5 minutes
Cooking time: 7-10 minutes
Makes a small pot

4 tbsp coriander seeds

2 tbsp cumin seeds

I tbsp fennel seeds

I tbsp uncooked basmati rice

I tsp black peppercorns

½ tsp fenugreek seeds

1-2 small dried red chillies

4 green cardamom pods

5 cloves

10 curry leaves (optional – you can
simply add these when you make the
curry, but I like to add them both in the
powder and the dish itself)

Roasted curry powder is known as Bathapu Thuna Paha in Sinhalese. This spice powder is commonly used with meat, fish, poultry and meat substitute dishes, although it can also be used in vegetarian curries to give a more intense, robust flavour. This powder is a lot darker in colour and more complex than the unroasted version, because it includes more spices and is heated for longer. Every household has its own unique version, and this is mine.

1. Warm a frying pan, then add all the ingredients and move them around the pan for a couple of minutes. The spices will release their aromas, giving off a wonderful scent, and will begin to darken as they roast.
2. Place everything in a spice grinder, including the rice and whole green cardamom pods. When the mixture has cooled, blitz to form a fine powder.
3. Store the powder in a sealed container in a cool dark place for up to 4 months.

Sri Lankan Unroasted Curry Powder

Preparation time: 5 minutes
Cooking time: 1-2 minutes
Makes a small pot

6 tbsp coriander seeds

3 tsp cumin seeds

3 tsp fennel seeds

Known as Thuna-Paha (three or five) in Sinhalese, unroasted or raw curry powder is commonly found in vegetarian dishes or dals in Sri Lanka. I tend to stick with three spices, but if you want to add two more to make the five, include a couple of curry leaves and a small cinnamon stick.

1. In a dry frying pan without any oil, roast all the ingredients on a low heat, moving them around the pan for I minute to release their fragrance and remove any moisture.
2. Transfer the spice mixture to a bowl and leave to cool, then place in a spice grinder and grind to a fine powder.
3. Store the powder in a sealed container in a cool dark place for up to 4 months.

North Indian Meat Masala Powder

Preparation time: 10 minutes
Cooking time: 5 minutes
Makes 50g

Masala simply means 'a blend of spices' and this one originates from North India with big, earthy spices such as coriander, cumin, cloves and cardamom dominating. There are South Indian meat masalas, which include different spices and ingredients such as fennel, fenugreek, coconut and curry leaves. Both are different from garam masala, which includes fewer spices. This works well with any meat, infusing your curry with wonderful aromas.

4 tbsp coriander seeds

2 tbsp cumin seeds

3 small dried red chillies

10 green cardamom pods

2 black cardamom pods

2 star anise

2 Indian bay leaves/tej patta

5cm (2 inches) cinnamon bark

10 cloves

½ a nutmeg

1 small mace flower

2 tsp whole black peppercorns

1. Put a heavy-based pan over a medium-low heat and when hot, add the coriander, cumin and dried red chillies.

2. After 30 seconds, add the rest of the ingredients and move them around the pan for a couple of minutes to release all the wonderful aromas. Be careful the heat isn't turned up too high as you do not want them to burn.

3. Transfer the spice mixture to a bowl and leave to cool, then use a spice grinder or pestle and mortar to grind into a fine powder.

4. Store the masala in a labelled glass jar and secure the lid firmly. Use within 3 months so that it remains fresh and aromatic.

Panch Phoron – Bengali Five Spice

Preparation time: 5 minutes
Makes 1 small jar

This Bengali five spice is nothing like the Chinese five spice. It is made up of cumin seeds, black or brown mustard seeds, nigella seeds, fennel seeds and fenugreek seeds in almost equal amounts. It is kept whole as opposed to being made into a powdered masala. Every home in Bengal will have this ubiquitous spice stored and ready to use. You can now pick it up in some large supermarkets or make your own and store it in a glass jar.

3 tbsp cumin seeds

3 tbsp nigella seeds

3 tbsp fennel seeds

3 tbsp black or brown mustard seeds

2 tbsp fenugreek seeds

1. Simply mix all the spices together in a bowl, then pour into a glass jar and seal.

2. Store in a cool place out of direct sunlight.

Ginger and Garlic Paste

Preparation time: 10 minutes
Makes 12 teaspoons

88g (approx. 10cm/4 inches) fresh ginger
2 whole garlic bulbs (23 cloves)
6 tbsp water
Pinch of salt

Notes: You can cook with this paste straight from frozen. Essentially, each cube is half ginger and half garlic, so if a recipe asks for 1 teaspoon of ginger and 1 teaspoon of garlic you could just add two cubes of this paste.

Typically, I just finely grate the required amount of fresh ginger and/or garlic for any given recipe. It takes so little time, is straightforward and almost forms a paste this way. If a recipe requires ginger-garlic paste, I grate equal amounts of both and then mix them together with a pinch of salt and a splash of water. You can of course use store-bought paste instead, which I occasionally revert to when I am in a hurry and gravitate towards the Sapna brand.

1. If you decide to leave the ginger unpeeled, give it a good wash first and then roughly chop. I tend to remove the skin with the back of a teaspoon, but it is totally fine to leave it on.

2. Break up the garlic bulbs and peel each of the cloves. Put the peeled cloves into a blender with the chopped ginger.

3. Add half the water and a pinch of salt to the blender, then blitz. Add the rest of the water to get the right consistency for your paste.

4. Transfer the ginger-garlic paste into ice cube trays, placing a teaspoon of it into each compartment. Place in the freezer, then transfer to a sealable bag once the cubes are solid. The paste lasts in the freezer for 1 month.

5. If you would rather store the paste in the fridge, transfer it to a sealed glass jar and pour a teaspoon of rapeseed oil (or a flavourless oil) on the top, which will help it last longer (about 1 week).

Ghee

Preparation time: 5 minutes
Cooking time: 35 minutes
Makes 1 jam jar

250g unsalted butter

Notes: Add a small dollop of ghee to hot rice or brush over chapati, naan or paratha. It also works well for tempering whole spices or garlic slithers before pouring over dal.

Making your own ghee is hugely satisfying. It is prepared by cooking the milk solids out of butter on a very low heat. The milk solids separate and settle at the bottom of the pan as the water evaporates. The resulting liquid is strained, and you are left with liquid gold, otherwise known as clarified butter. According to Ayurvedic customs (traditional medicine practiced in India), it aids digestion. I use it sparingly as a delicious indulgence, as opposed to eating it every day.

1. Heat a small pan and put the whole block of butter into it. Keep the heat very low for the next 30 minutes. The butter will melt slowly, and foam will begin to form. Do not touch the butter or the pan yet. It will bubble away until it's ready, so listen for this sound stopping.

2. After 30 minutes, there will be a lot of foam on the surface of the butter and the bubbling sound will have ceased. Turn off the heat, then carefully skim off the foam and discard it.

3. Allow the ghee to cool, then pour it through a fine strainer lined with a muslin or cheesecloth into a sterilised glass jar for storage. Leave to cool, uncovered.

4. Once the strained ghee has cooled completely, place the lid on the jar. The colour will be a beautiful clear honey yellow, then as it hardens it will become a more mellow yellow.

5. The ghee can be kept at room temperature away from light and heat for 1-2 months, or for longer in the fridge.

Menu Ideas

While many of the dishes in this book can be eaten on their own, they are often best alongside one or two other dishes. Typically in India, dishes are eaten in a sequence. A meal begins with dal and rice or flatbreads, followed by a few vegetable dishes. You may then be offered a fish or shellfish course, and this could even be followed by a meat course. To finish would be something sweet. You eat small portions of everything, much in the same way that Spanish tapas works. Together it all makes a very satisfying meal. Other than for special dinners, I don't necessarily cook a meat and fish curry in the same sitting, instead opting for one or the other (or none) and then accompanying them with a couple of vegetable curries and always a dal. When I state that a recipe is for 4 people it is expected that you would select one or two other dishes to complement it. There are some recipes that amount to a standalone meal though, such as mussel molee or Himalayan chicken thukpa.

I have provided some ideas for various occasions below, which I hope will provide inspiration as to what dishes work well together and what to cook in every situation. There are no set rules and I quite often mix dishes from North, South, East and West India. I try and make the plate colourful and inviting, so typically won't cook recipes that are all the same colours. The more you cook from this book, the better your appreciation of what works well for you will be.

Midweek Suppers
Speedy Salmon Curry with Lemon Rice
Bengali Mustard Fish Curry with Basmati Rice
Chilli Garlic Mackerel with Fine Green Bean Thoran and Chapati
Mussel Molee with Lemon Rice
Turmeric and Nigella Seed Bream Fry with Dill Dal and Basmati Rice
Tuna Fish Bora with Kachumber Salad and Sri Lankan Coconut Dal
Himalayan Chicken Thukpa
Lamb Keema with Chapati or Naan

Speedy Lunches
Ginger and Lemongrass Prawn Bisque
Black-Eyed Beans with Tamarind and Coconut
Chickpea Pancakes with Bengali Tomato Chutney
Avial
Rasam
Cherry Tomato Masoor Dal
Butternut Yellow Mung Dal

হিন্দু হোটেল HIN
7B DACRES LANE, K
MENU মেনু
ICE WITH DAL ভাত ডাল
AL ডাল
VEGETABLE সবজী
RY ভাজা
ALOO CHOKHA আলু চোখা
SPL.VEGE ABLE স্পেশাল সবজী
MURO GHANTO মুড়ো ঘন্টো
FISH KALIA মাছের কালিয়া
FISH CURR মাছের ঝোল
FISH BATA বাটা মাছ
FISH ELISH ইলিশ মাছ
FISH TALAPIA তেলাপিয়া মাছ
FISH BHOLA ভোলা মাছ
EGG CURRY ডিমের কারী
EGG KASSA ডিমের কষা
EGG OMLET ডিমের ওমলেট
MUTTON KASSA কষা মাংস
MUTTON CURRY কারী মাংস
CHICKEN KASSA কষা মুরগী
CHICKEN CURRY কারী মুরগী
EGG TARKA ডিম তড়কা
FRY TARKA ফ্রাই তড়কা
PLAIN TARKA প্লেন তড়কা
DAL FRY ডাল ফ্রাই
ROTI রুটি
CHATTNI চাটনী
ACHAR
PARCEL

Vegan

Bengali Green Bean and Potato Curry with Coconut and Sultana Chana Dal and Sweet Potato Tikki

Potato, Pea and Paneer Curry with Fine Green Bean Thoran and Sri Lankan Coconut Dal

Unripe Jackfruit Curry

Keralan Cauliflower and Coconut Milk Curry

Aubergine and Tamarind Curry

Spiced Smoky Aubergine

Rasam

Budget Friendly

Bengali Egg Curry

Courgette and Tomato Curry with Chapati

Nigella Seed, Sprout and Carrot Curry

Chilli Garlic Mackerel

Squid Coconut Fry

Hot and Sour Rasam Soup

Mussel Molee

Cauliflower with Potato and Dried Fenugreek

Butternut Yellow Mung Dal

Chicken Liver Curry

Palak Dal

Unripe Jackfruit Curry

Coconut and Sultana Chana Dal

Dhaba Style Dal Fry

Green Mung, Garlic and Tomato Dal

Dill Dal

Cherry Tomato Masoor Dal

Black-Eyed Beans with Tamarind and Coconut

Punjabi Chole

Rajma

Sambar

Sri Lankan Coconut Dal

Leisurely Weekend Lunches

Egg Appam with Spicy Caramelised Onion Sambol and Sambar

Chickpea Pancakes with Bengali Tomato Chutney

Turmeric and Nigella Seed Bream Fry with Chaat Salad and Sri Lankan Coconut Dal

Chicken Kathi Rolls with Coriander, Mint and Lime Chutney

Spiced Smoky Aubergine with Palak Dal and Paratha

Rava or Green Goddess Dosa with Aloo Bhaji and South Indian Tomato and Date Chutney

Mussel Molee

Aubergine and Tamarind Curry with Paratha

Family Meals

Homestyle Bengali Chicken Curry, Cauliflower with Potato and Dried Fenugreek and Cherry Tomato Masoor Dal

Lamb Keema with Keralan Cabbage Thoran and Chapati

Lamb Rogan Josh with Nigella Seed, Sprout and Carrot Curry and Naan Bread

Chicken Methi Malai with Keralan Cabbage Thoran and Naan Bread

Cashew and Tomato Chicken Curry with Beetroot Curry and Chapati or Lemon Rice

Bengali Lamb Chop Curry, Cauliflower with Potato and Dried Fenugreek, Palak Dal and Chapati

Speedy Salmon Curry with Butternut Yellow Mung Dal or Palak Dal and Bengali Green Bean and Potato Curry

Keralan Fish Molee with Courgette, Potato and Pea Sabzi and Lemon Rice

Turmeric and Nigella Seed Bream Fry with Palak Dal and Fine Green Bean Thoran

Bengali Egg Curry with Green Mung, Garlic and Tomato Dal and Lemon Rice

Light Meals

Green Mung, Garlic and Tomato Dal

Himalayan Chicken Thukpa

Dill Dal

Tuna Fish Bora with Kachumber Salad or Cherry Tomato Masoor Dal

Kachumber Salad with Sweet Potato Tikki and Tamarind and Date Chutney

Bengali Mustard Fish Curry with Basmati Rice

Mussel Molee

Rava Dosa with Aloo Bhaji and Coconut Chutney

Sri Lankan Coconut Dal

Egg Appam with South Indian Tomato and Date Chutney

Black-Eyed Beans with Tamarind and Coconut

Keralan Cauliflower and Coconut Milk Curry

Courgette and Tomato Curry

Speedy Salmon Curry

Guests for Tea

Masala Chai with the following:

Dhokla

Red Onion Pakora with South Indian Tomato and Date Chutney

Indian Savoury Doughnuts with Coriander, Mint and Lime Chutney

Daler Bora

Dinner Parties for 6-8

To Start: Red Onion Pakora or Daler Bora with Coriander, Mint and Lime Chutney/South Indian Tomato and Date Chutney/Tamarind and Date Chutney OR Spiced Okra Munchies

Keralan Coconut Chicken Curry, Okra Sabzi, Palak Dal and Lemon Rice, followed by Chocolate, Chilli and Cinnamon Fondants with Cardamom Cream

Opium Chicken, Rajma, Spicy Potato Curry, Keralan Cauliflower and Coconut Milk Curry and Beetroot Paratha, followed by Strawberry and Black Pepper Kulfi

Tamarind Prawn Curry, Sri Lankan Coconut Dal, Potato, Pea and Paneer Curry and Chapati, followed by Cinnamon and Nutmeg Panna Cotta with Raspberry Coulis

Prawn Malai Curry, Fine Green Bean Thoran, White Cabbage with Fennel Seeds and Sultanas, Green Mung, Garlic and Tomato Dal and Lemon Rice, followed by Chilli and Mint Choc Chip Ice Cream

Bengali Lamb Chop Curry, Bengali Green Bean and Potato Curry, Butternut Yellow Mung Dal and Basmati Rice or Naan, followed by Chaat Masala Fruit Salad

Keralan Cauliflower with Coconut Milk Curry, Fine Green Bean Thoran, Potato, Pea and Paneer Curry, Dill Dal and Basmati Rice, followed by Tropical Pavlova with Cardamom Cream

Aubergine and Tamarind Curry, Courgette, Potato and Pea Sabzi, Nigella Seed, Sprout and Carrot Curry, Palak Dal, Bengali Tomato Chutney and Naan or Chapati followed by Chilli and Mint Choc Chip Ice Cream

Some Like it Hot

Hot and Sour Rasam Soup

Chettinad Pepper Chicken

Goan Pork Vinadaloo

Spicy Potato Curry

Late Night Munchies

Fried White Poppy Seed Aubergine

Crispy Cumin Potatoes

Spiced Okra Munchies

Indian Style Scrambled Eggs

Indian Eggy Bread

Spice Suppliers

While large supermarkets in the UK are increasingly widening their spice offering, I find a lot of online suppliers are excellent at covering a wide array of spices that will give your cooking authentic flavour. You can order online from most of the suppliers listed below. Here's a sample of the ones I use or hear good things about.

UK Suppliers

Bhavin's Food
A few doors down from Patel Brothers. Not online yet, but worth a visit if you are in Tooting for their friendly welcome and the wide array of fresh produce.
193-197 Upper Tooting Road, London SW17 7TG

Hallan's Cash and Carry
Based in Sussex, this cash and carry has a wide range of spices and fresh produce. They also have an online offering.
www.somayaskitchen.co.uk
63 Ifield Road, Crawley, West Sussex RH11 7AS

Korea Foods
As the name suggests, the focus here is more towards Korean, Japanese and Chinese food products, but it does have a good selection of Indian spices. It also stocks fresh pandan (rampa) leaves, which you can freeze for later use. The place is huge and has everything from live fish to fresh Korean food you can buy for your lunch.
www.koreafoods.co.uk
Wyvern Industrial Estate, 4 Unit 5, Beverley Way, New Malden KT3 4PH

Little India
If you are in southwest London, go seek out Little India, next to Patel Brothers. It is an Aladdin's Cave of Indian pots, pans, incense, pestles and mortars, tawas, tiffin tins, and everything you could possibly want to begin your Indian culinary journey. Mention that Torie from Chilli and Mint sent you and I'm sure you'll be greeted with a big smile!
191 Upper Tooting Road, London SW17 7TG

Patel Brothers
Family-run business established four decades ago; the younger generation have taken the reins and are very helpful if you go in person. Spices, lentils, flours and rice: you name it, they probably stock it. You can also find your fresh curry leaves here, or dried if you are ordering online.
www.asiandukan.co.uk
187-189 Upper Tooting Road, London SW17 7TG

Red Rickshaw
The largest Indian online grocery store in the UK. It literally stocks everything you require to become a spice wizard. It also has all those fresh ingredients that are hard to source. Worth checking out if you become stuck for ingredients.
www.redrickshaw.com

Rooted Spices

Carefully sourced for the best taste, freshness and potency with a focus on single origin spices. The spices arrive in elegant blue tins that can be bought on their own or as part of a gift box. Online only.

www.rootedspices.com

Sous Chef

Stocks a wide range of global ingredients and cooking equipment for the home cook and professional kitchen.

www.souschef.co.uk

The Asian Cookshop

This online spice shop sells literally thousands of spices, so if you struggle to find what you are after they are bound to have it.

www.theasiancookshop.co.uk

The Spice Shop

Based in Notting Hill on Blenheim Crescent, as well as Gardner Street in Brighton, The Spice Shop has a wide range of herbs and spices, as well as spice blends. The Notting Hill branch is positioned opposite the famous Books for Cooks bookshop so it's worth going in person if you are in the neighbourhood. You can also order online.

www.thespiceshop.co.uk

1 Blenheim Crescent, London W11 2EE and 10 Gardner Street, Brighton BN1 1UP

US Suppliers

Burlap & Barrell

Whenever I am in the US, I always place an order here as their spices really are magnificent. The hugely knowledgeable founders, Ethan and Ori, set up in 2016. Online only and available to those in the US and Canada, although I am hoping their reach will extend to the UK soon.

www.burlapandbarrel.com

Kalustyans

If you are based state-side, Kalustyans on Lexington Avenue in Manhattan is a landmark for spices, condiments and for all those ingredients you wonder where on earth to source. They have been operating since 1944 so are definitely worth a visit. They also deliver nationwide in the US.

www.kalustyans.com

123 Lexington Avenue, New York, NY 10016

Acknowledgements

Many people have helped me evolve my seed of an idea into this beautiful cook book.

I could not have asked for a more professional and straightforward team to collaborate with than Meze Publishing. Thanks to Phil Turner, managing director, for supporting me and my vision from the outset. My superb editor Katie Fisher was a dream to work with. Creative director Paul Cocker's creativity brought this book to life. Emma Toogood and Lizzy Capps excelled at promoting this book around the UK and beyond.

Photography is key with any cook book, bringing the recipes to life and enticing the reader. Tim Green was a perfect partner. A talented and experienced photographer, he brought perspective and patience as well as some great props. After cooking and shooting through the hottest days of summer, I now know that anything is possible!

My team of recipe testers deserve a special mention. Thank you to the willing volunteers from the Guild of Food Writers: Christopher Trotter, Sarah Giles, Christie Dietz, Amy Bates, Jenny Hammerton, Susan Low, Lizzie Crow, Vritti Bansal, Brooke Jackson, Judy Ridgway, Paul Bellchambers, Kacie Morgan, Fanny Charles and Amanda Clegg. I am very grateful for all your insight and feedback. Thanks also go to Natasha Joseph, Sohini Badiani, Lindsay Telling, Sophie and Percy Banks, Rasna Ubhi, John Werritty, Catja Thum, Helen Gambarota and Charlotte Averdick.

Thank you to my friends who lent me props for the shoot, as well as Eleanor Khan who kindly gifted me a few items from her beautiful online store Nimuri, and to China and Co where I spent many a happy hour in their Aladdin's cave of props.

My thanks also extend to the many people who signed up for my cookery classes over the years. I have so enjoyed meeting all of you and appreciated your support. A special thanks though to Alice Fontana, Monique Tollgard, Benedikte Malling, Lucy Smith, Kate Cawdron, Ingrid Fox and Simona Barbieri who have all helped me spread the word and supported my ventures over the years, and to Gina Chamier and Dearbhla Fidler who encouraged me to start teaching others how to cook Indian food a number of years ago. Thank you for setting me off on this journey.

My mother-in-law, Swapna, and my Indian family deserve a big thank you for introducing me to all the wonderful offerings in the Bengali culinary repertoire. It has been immensely enjoyable immersing myself in authentic, delicious food over the years. Trips to Kolkata are always electric and the hospitality and warmth is second to none.

Thank you to my loving parents for their continual support and encouragement. My love of food, spice and the exotic definitely came from hearing their tales of travels around Africa, India and central Asia in the 1970s, combined with all their culinary creations over the years. My sister Rowena and brother-in-law Jasper, along with my brother Al and sister-in-law Flora, were all immensely helpful in testing some of the recipes and providing constructive feedback.

My final thanks go to my husband, Indy, and daughters Allegra and Zinnia who have all helped me bring this book to life. I could not wish for a more positive trio who have encouraged and supported me throughout this project.

Index

Chana dal

Aloo Bhaji - Spiced Potato 32

Coconut and Sultana Chana Dal 66

Lemon Rice 174

Coconut Chutney 188

South Indian Tomato and Date Chutney 188

Carrot Chutney 190

Sambar Masala 214

Cherry tomatoes

Cherry Tomato Masoor Dal 70

Chicken

Chicken Kathi Rolls 58

Himalayan Chicken Thukpa 76

Chettinad Pepper Chicken 150

Chicken Liver Curry 152

Chicken Methi Malai 154

Homestyle Bengali Chicken Curry 160

Keralan Coconut Chicken Curry 162

Opium Chicken 170

Chickpeas

Chaat Salad 56

Punjabi Chole 82

Chocolate

Chilli and Mint Choc Chip Ice Cream 196

Chocolate, Chilli and Cinnamon Fondants 202

Cocoa powder

Chocolate, Chilli and Cinnamon Fondants 202

Coconut cream

Keralan Coconut Chicken Curry 162

Coconut milk

Appam 34

Black-Eyed Beans with Tamarind and Coconut 64

Sri Lankan Coconut Dal 85

Aubergine and Tamarind Curry 92

Keralan Cauliflower and Coconut Milk Curry 94

Beetroot Curry 98

Avial 124

Keralan Fish Molee 132

Prawn Malai Curry 136

Mussel Molee 138

Keralan Coconut Chicken Curry 162

Cod

Keralan Fish Molee 132

Prawn Malai Curry 136

Tamarind Prawn Curry 144

Condensed milk

Strawberry and Black Pepper Kulfi 208

Courgette

Cherry Tomato Masoor Dal 70

Courgette and Tomato Curry 90

Courgette, Potato and Pea Sabzi 110

Cucumber

Kachumber Salad 50

Chaat Salad 56

Chicken Kathi Rolls 58

Pomegranate Raita 186

D

Dates

South Indian Tomato and Date Chutney 188

Bengali Tomato Chutney 191

Tamarind and Date Chutney 192

Desiccated coconut

Fine Green Bean Thoran 112

Keralan Cabbage Thoran 114

Avial 124

Bengali Prawn Curry 130

Naan Bread 178

Carrot Chutney 190

Dijon mustard

Bengali Mustard Fish Curry 128

Double cream

Chicken Methi Malai 154

Chilli and Mint Choc Chip Ice Cream 196

Panna Cotta with Raspberry Coulis 204

Strawberry and Black Pepper Kulfi 208

Tropical Pavlova with Cardamom Cream 210

Drumstick

Sambar 86

Avial 124

Written by: Torie True

Edited by: Katie Fisher, Phil Turner

Photography by: Tim Green

Location photography: Torie True

Food & Prop Styling: Torie True, Tim Green

Designed by: Paul Cocker, Lucy Godbold

PR: Emma Toogood, Lizzy Capps

Contributors: Katherine Dullforce, Lis Ellis
Michael Johnson, Lizzie Morton

Printed and bound in the UK by
Bell & Bain Ltd, Glasgow

@chilliandmint
www.chilliandmint.com

MIX
Paper from
responsible sources
FSC® C007785

Published by Meze Publishing Limited
Unit 1b, 2 Kelham Square
Kelham Riverside
Sheffield S3 8SD
Web: www.mezepublishing.co.uk
Telephone: 0114 275 7709
Email: info@mezepublishing.co.uk